FLYING TIGER ARCHIVES

volume 2
1966-1989

Guy Van Herbruggen

designed by Simon De Rudder
edited by Charles Kennedy & Sue Blunt

Acknowledgements

Welcome to the second volume of the Flying Tiger archives, focusing on the period from 1966 to 1989. This book, a continuation of the previous volume which covered the early years from 1945 to 1965, presents a chronological journey through the last twenty-four years of the Flying Tiger Line (FTL).

Within these pages, you will find a curated collection of the finest photographs sourced from the Flying Tiger Line Historical Society (FTLHS) archives, along with exceptional slide scans from various collections, beginning with the collection of the esteemed Jacques Guillem. It is important to acknowledge Jacques, a dear friend and mentor, who passed away on April 1, 2023.

I extend my gratitude to Peter Van Leeuw and Frank de Koster for their invaluable assistance in enhancing challenging slide scans through Photoshop.

This book owes much to the contributions of others. I express sincere thanks to Thomas Livesey for generously sharing Jon Proctor's Flying Tiger photo collection, Andreas van Loon for the FTL 707s from his extensive slide collection, and Thomas Robert Singfield for his contributions. Additionally, retired Flight Attendant Kenneth Barton provided invaluable insights and photographs on Flying Tigers and Metro International passenger operations.

A heartfelt thank you goes to everyone at the FTLHS for their unwavering support, passion for the airline, and contributions to this book. John Dickson, in his dual role as President of the Flying Tiger Line Pilots Association (FTLPA) and the FTLHS, has been particularly instrumental. Special mention goes to John Burke, President of the Flying Tiger Club (FTC), Helena Burke, Vice-President of the FTC, and Marshall Meyers, Attorney and son of FTL General Counsel. Special thanks to George Gewehr, FTLPA Historian, who helped me over the last year and found answers to my questions.

I would like to acknowledge the individuals who provided photographic material, information, or shared their personal archives: Robert Baird, Lou Borok, Marilyn Breen, Lee Churchman, Joyce Danielsen, Jean-Claude Démirdjian, Colleen Ferguson, Josie Gibson, Archie Hall, Pamela Hunter, Erich Krueck, Terri Lane, Bob Lane, Annette Lusk, Gary Molinari, Paul Nowaske, Debbie Paul, Robin Pestarino, Leslie Pfeifer, Lynne R. Rayner, Debbi Rickman, Lydia Rossi, Jane Stoecklin, John "Tym" Tymczyszyn, Glenn Van Winkle, Christian Volpati, Gary Whitesides, and Rosemary Zettler.

A heartfelt thank you to Helena and John Burke for their hospitality during my visits to LAX, where I delved into the FTLHS archives.

Special gratitude is reserved for my best friend, Charles Kennedy, for his invaluable editorial assistance, insight, and unwavering support. I am grateful for his dedication, which ensures the preservation of our legacy for future generations.

I must also acknowledge Simon de Rudder for his patience and dedication to the book's design.

Thanks to Astral Horizon Press, particularly Bhavna Vadher, Steve Finnigan, Mathew Butler, and Sebastian Schmitz, for their ongoing support as my publisher.

Last but certainly not least, my profound appreciation goes to my wife, France, whose support and understanding were indispensable throughout the book's creation. Without her, this project would not have been possible.

I trust you will find as much enjoyment in reading this book as I did in producing it.

Guy Van Herbruggen
March 2024

FLYING TIGER ARCHIVES
Volume two, 1966 - 1989
Guy Van Herbruggen
ISBN 978-1-7396630-4-9
© 2024 Astral Horizon Aviation Press. All rights reserved.
www.theairlineboutique.com   www.astralhorizon.co.uk

Preface

Guy's second volume delves into the course of the Flying Tiger Line's history from 1966 to 1989, a period marked as the Jet Age in the travel industry. Already distinguished with Canadair CL-44s and Boeing 707s, the carrier's expansion into 1970s was propelled by the introduction of the stretched Douglas DC-8-63 in June 1969.

The 1970s was witness to a shrinking globe, with Flying Tigers strategically capitalising on opportunities, including substantial commitment in the Military Airlift Command (MAC) program and the Civil Reserve Air Fleet (CRAF) during the Vietnam conflict. The incorporation of Boeing 747 Freight Master in 1974 significantly boosted fleet capacity for longer routes. The subsequent acquisition of 747-200Fs featuring unique nose loading capabilities solidified the airline's commitment to transporting Anything, Anytime, Anywhere. In 1979, FTL surpassed Pan Am to become the world's leading air cargo carrier and it appeared that nothing could get in the way of continued profitability.

Nevertheless, the tide turned with the deregulation of the domestic all-cargo industry in November 1977, a change founder Robert Prescott had vehemently opposed. Shortly after battling for the airline that he created, the founder and President of the Flying Tiger Line passed away on March 3, 1978.

The 1980s brought turmoil and substantial losses within Tiger International Holding Inc's subsidiaries led by CEO Wayne Hoffman, ironically a vocal advocate of deregulation. The merger with Seaboard World Airlines in October 1981 expanded operations into Europe but came at an enormous cost. Ambitious overexpansion, high interest rates, fuel price increases, and the negative impacts of deregulation led to sustained financial losses.

An attempt to enter the express package business with Boeing 727-100s in the 1980s, mirroring FedEx's hub-and-spoke system, proved insufficient to rescue Flying Tigers from its financial decline. In December 1988, Federal Express Corporation announced its acquisition of Tiger International, leading to a separate operational existence until the successful merger on August 7, 1989. The poignant final chapter to FTL's story early 1989 was marked by the tragic crash of a Boeing 747 near Kuala Lumpur.

Post-merger, Joe Baker, long-time Tiger employee and President of the Tiger Retirement Club supervised preservation efforts of Flying Tiger Line memorabilia in two rooms in the former Sam Mosher training building across from the Los Angeles FedEx Heavy Maintenance Hangar. However, in mid-2023, the termination of FedEx's lease necessitated relocation of the archives, leading to the formation of the Flying Tiger Line Historical Society, to preserve the airline's legacy. The society's mission is to maintain a digital repository for aviation enthusiasts and students to share the Flying Tiger Line's history and educate about its role in air cargo and charter flights. For more information, visit www.FTLHS.org.

Captain John Dickson, FTL, FDX, ret.
President, Flying Tiger Line Historical Society
President, Flying Tiger Line Pilots Association

Winter in Alaska. Second Officer Tom Constable supplied these two photographs of Flying Tiger Line Lockheed L-1049H N6918C, covered with snow, and Canadair CL-44 N450T, parked on a wintery tarmac, in front of the Tiger cargo terminal in Anchorage, on a crisp January day in 1966.
Tom Constable

Flying Tiger Line - El Al operation. The Boeing 707-358B, with the registration 4X-ATR, was built and delivered to El Al on January 7, 1966. However, on the very same day, it entered into a lease agreement with the Flying Tiger Line as N317F due to a strike by El Al's crew. This rare photograph, taken on January 13, 1966 at the Lockheed Air Terminal (Burbank Airport), depicts the aircraft during this unique leasing arrangement while still wearing complete El Al livery, before the addition of Flying Tiger Line titles.

Jacques Guillem Collection

Bird's eye. Two Canadair 44D4-2 turboprops, with their fuselages opened, were being prepared for loading on the ramp at the Flying Tiger Line cargo terminal in Los Angeles.

Jon Proctor Collection

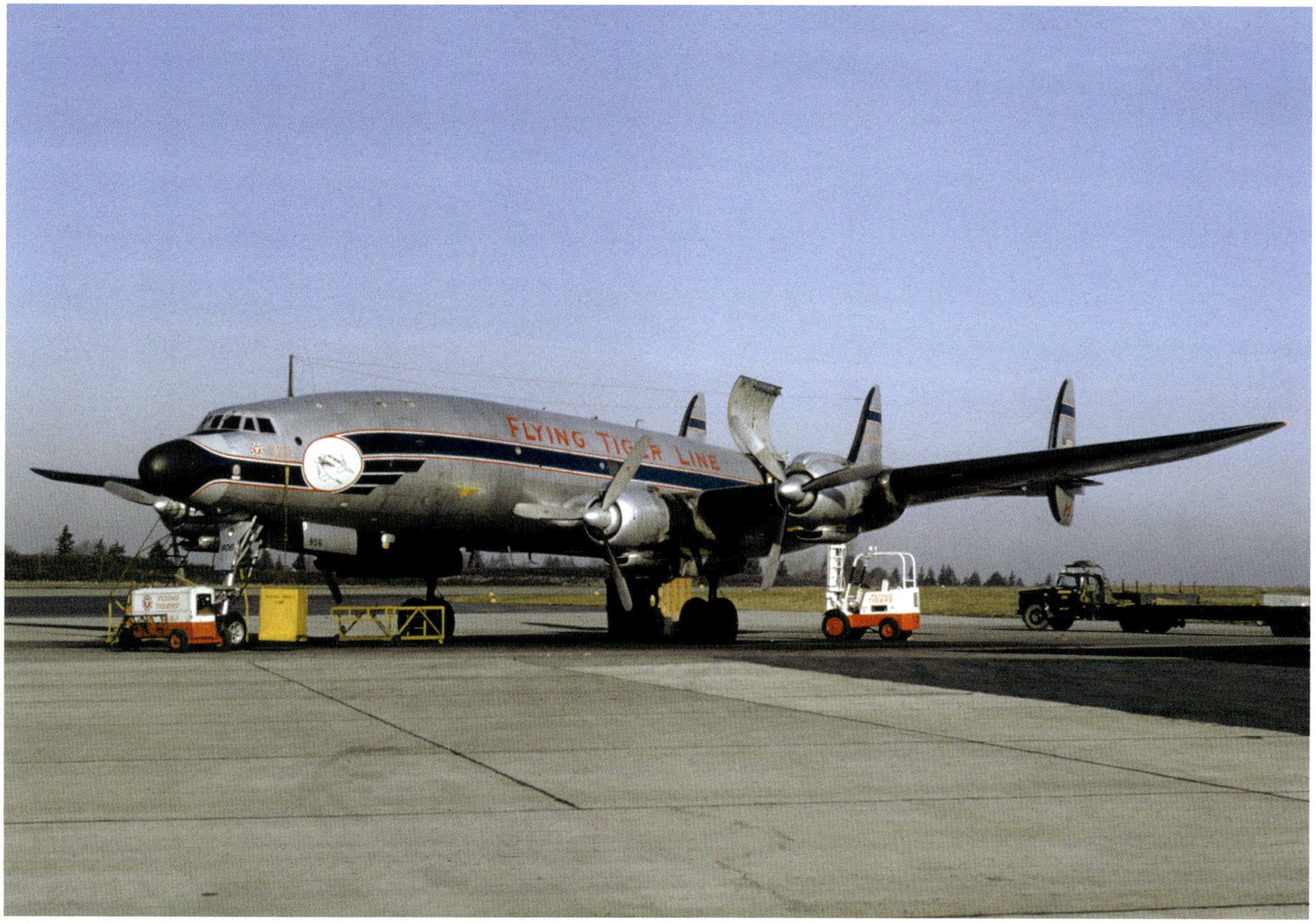

The dawn of the Constellation. By March 1966, N6916C was among the eight remaining L-1049H Constellations in the Flying Tiger fleet. The CL-44s began replacing the Connies starting in 1962. In June 1966, seven L-1049H aircraft were transferred to a subsidiary, Flying Tiger Air Services, which conducted charter operations in the Southeast Asia region from 1966 to 1967. By mid-1968, N6916C was placed in storage at Kingman, Arizona, where it was eventually dismantled for spare parts in either 1973 or 1974. *Jacques Guillem Collection*

Bye Bye Burbank. In January 1966, Joe E. Baker, Manager of Facilities and Equipment, played a significant role in orchestrating the move of Tigers' headquarters from Lockheed Air Terminal (Burbank Airport) to Los Angeles International Airport. Despite his busy schedule, he successfully organised the transfer of 850 employees and approximately 1,750 tons of equipment and machinery. The move marked the completion of a facility transfer that began in 1964 when the Tigers established their freight station at Los Angeles International Airport. Baker's dedication and efforts were crucial in ensuring a smooth relocation from Burbank, where the Tigers had been based since 1947. Delmar Watson Photos

New Home for the Tigers. Flying Tiger Line's new $4.5 million world headquarters in Los Angeles, located at 7401 World Way West, featured a modern office building in the front and large hangar and equipment buildings at the rear. Over 1,000 employees, previously working in a chaotic facility in Burbank, now enjoyed the 38,000 square foot, two-storey office building, and the region's largest cantilever maintenance hangar. The new facilities included spacious reception areas, air-conditioning, an advanced IBM computer department, a modern print shop, and a cafeteria for 180 people. The parking area accommodated 550 cars, while the vast hangar could house three Boeing 707s wingtip to wingtip during maintenance and overhaul.

Hangar dedicated. On March 25, 1966, a ceremony dedicated the new Flying Tiger Line facility, boasting the largest cantilever hangar west of Atlanta. Robert W. Prescott introduced Bill Bartling, Tiger's VP of Planning and Research, during the event. The festive occasion celebrated the employees, including Joe Baker (employee 0020) who joined in 1945. At the gala, Baker humorously remarked, "Back in Long Beach, I could throw a baseball over the garage backward. In this new building, the best hitter today couldn't hit a fly ball from wall to wall, a distance of over 480 feet." In the background, notable aircraft include Boeing 707-358B N317F leased from El Al, a Learjet 23 N460F, and the engines used in the 1966 fleet: L-1049H Wright R-3350 turbo-compound, 707-349C Pratt & Whitney JT3D-3, and CL-44D4-2 Rolls-Royce Tyne turboprops.

Grateful group. Around 100 Korean orphans, now with American foster parents, gathered at the Flying Tiger cafeteria in Los Angeles for a special birthday celebration in April 1966. They had arrived in the United States aboard Boeing 707-358B N317F. Instead of receiving gifts, these thoughtful children decided to reverse the norm and sent presents to their siblings who remained in the Seoul orphanage. In the centre of the picture are Kwang Soo Ahn, Consul General of South Korea and Captain Robert H. "Bob" Martin.

Hawaiian Holiday. From May 29 to June 14, 1966, a series of five passenger charter flights bound for Honolulu were conducted by the Flying Tiger Line on behalf of Philco, utilising Boeing 707-349Cs N322F and N323F. N322F is depicted in the photograph taken on May 29 in Honolulu. Philco, a renowned American electronics manufacturer headquartered in Philadelphia, made significant contributions in battery, radio, and television production. Noteworthy among its achievements, in 1963, Philco played a pivotal role in the creation, production, installation, and maintenance of all consoles utilised in both Mission Operations Control Rooms, commonly known as Mission Control, within Building 30 of NASA's Lyndon B. Johnson Space Center situated in Houston, Texas. These consoles were instrumental in the management of missions spanning Gemini, Apollo, Skylab, and the Space Shuttle programs until 1998. The consoles designed and implemented by Philco for Mission Control 2 at the Johnson Space Center have been meticulously preserved, and the control room itself holds a distinguished place in the National Register of Historic Places under the name "Apollo Mission Control Center".

Fourth Tiger Seven-O-Seven. N324F was the fourth Boeing 707 delivered and leased to the Flying Tiger Line on June 21, 1966. The photograph captures the brand new aircraft positioned in front of the newly constructed maintenance hangar in Los Angeles.

Flying Tiger Line - El Al operation. Boeing 707-358B N317F of the Flying Tiger Line was under lease to El Al, with Tiger cockpit and cabin crew, owing to a strike by El Al's crew from January to October 1966. The aircraft was subsequently returned to El Al and re-registered as 4X-ATR. This photo was captured during Summer 1966 at Rome - Fiumicino Airport, taken during a scheduled El Al flight originating from Tel Aviv. Jacques Guillem Collection

Seaboard World leasing. Flying Tiger Line's Canadair CL-44 N455T was spotted at London Heathrow in August 1966 during its lease to Seaboard World Airlines. Initially built for Tiger, it had its maiden flight on July 11, 1961, and was officially delivered on July 23, 1961.
Jon Proctor Collection

180,000 pounds of Tiger lift at Newark. Photography, Inc.

Around the world in seven days. On September 13, 1966, Captain Ken Henderson flew N447T from Newark to Philadelphia, where a planeload of tents awaited shipment to the Agency for International Development (AID). AID had taken a significant role in aiding those affected by the devastating earthquake in Varto, Turkey, which claimed over 2,394 lives and injured up to 1,500 people on August 19. The Tigers' involvement extended beyond this tent charter, as the nine-man crew would embark on a 28,500-mile journey around the world, covering 75 total flight hours in just over a week. In addition to Captain Henderson, the crew included Captain C. Monte "Monty" Treft, co-pilot Pete Prichard, flight engineers John Ladonisi and John Graco, navigators Hank Clark and Harry Myers, along with Walt Wilkinson (flight mechanic) and Joe Barbera (agent). Their first fuel stop was in Shannon, Ireland, followed by heading southeast across Europe to Turkish capital Ankara, where the tents were offloaded and received by the AID Mission.

Captain Ken Henderson and Co-pilot Armstead "Pete" M. Prichard en route to Ankara.

Following a brief turnaround in Ankara, the aircraft proceeded to Torino, Italy, to pick up missile components destined for Woomera, Australia. The crew finally had the opportunity to rest in Torino, arriving at approximately 4 a.m. local time on September 15. This marked their first break since departing Philadelphia. Loaded with three oversized and custom-shaped crates, the '44 departed Torino for Rome to collect an additional 5,000 pounds of cargo intended for Woomera. However, an incident occurred at Fiumicino Airport during the opening of the CL-44's swingtail. The left rear horizontal elevator collided with the stair stand, causing damage to the control tab. This setback necessitated a delay for repairs, as shown in the top picture. Despite the unexpected hiccup, the damaged control tab was rebuilt by Alitalia maintenance personnel. This delay pushed the departure from Rome to Colombo until the morning of the 16th. The journey included technical stops in Beirut (as seen in the centre picture) and Damascus before embarking on the long leg to Colombo. Upon landing in Colombo, a blown tire was promptly replaced by Walt Wilkinson. Following an uneventful 10-hour flight across the Indian Ocean, the aircraft arrived in Perth, Australia. There, personnel from the Italian-Australian missile launching project unloaded the Fiat parts and the special rocket booster, as shown in the bottom picture. A swift turnaround took the CL-44 on its way, departing for Brisbane and then Honolulu before commencing the final leg of its round-the-world journey back to Los Angeles. The plane touched down in Los Angeles on September 20 at 4 p.m.

Precise loading. In September 1966, a significant operation took place at Boston, as a mighty 38,000-pound gas turbine was carefully loaded onto the Canadair CL-44 N447T aircraft bound for Puerto Rico. This gas turbine represented a critical piece of machinery, destined for a power generation facility on the island. The precise loading process required skilled personnel and meticulous coordination to ensure the turbine's safe transportation. John R. Gallagher

Lockheed Super Starlifters: From commercial ambition to NASA. In 1964, Flying Tigers placed a surprising $64 million order for eight massive Lockheed L-300 Super Starlifters, based on the C-141A as used by the Military Air Transport Service (MATS) and stretched by 37 feet, 11 m. The L-300 prototype, registered N4141A, underwent modifications to be better suited to commercial use. In late 1966, N4141A was displayed on the Flying Tiger ramp in Los Angeles, where direct loading tests were conducted for Tiger's engineers and customers. Despite Lockheed's efforts to market the aircraft to civilian operators, only provisional orders were placed by Flying Tiger Line and Slick Airways, leading to the construction of a single civilian demonstration aircraft. When L-300 programme was dropped, Lockheed delivered the sole aircraft to NASA's Ames Research Center, operating as N714NA out of Moffett Field, California. Outfitted with a 36-inch (91.5 cm) telescope, it was dedicated as the Gerard P. Kuiper Airborne Observatory (KAO) on May 21, 1975. This telescope facilitated infrared astronomy at altitudes up to 45,000 feet. The aircraft remained in service until its retirement in 1995 when it was replaced by the SOFIA Boeing 747SP. Above picture shows Lockheed demonstrator L-300-50A StarLifter N4141A at Mascot, Sydney on 27 August 1966. Jacques Guillem Collection

First DC-8-63 rolled out. The Douglas DC-8-63 made its debut at the Long Beach plant of Douglas Aircraft Company on March 6, 1967, amidst a grand celebration featuring a band of bagpipers and a distinguished audience composed of airline presidents and executives from the aircraft industry. One prominent figure present was Robert W. Prescott, who placed an order for ten aircraft, worth $105 million, with an option for four more. Also attending the roll-out ceremony was Tom Haywood, supervisor of Flying Tiger's technical training department within Flight Operations. The event held special significance for both Prescott and Haywood, as nearly 22 years earlier, the first flights of the Flying Tiger Line (National Skyways Freight Corporation at the time) from the same field, Long Beach Municipal Airport. Prescott couldn't contain his excitement as he remarked to Haywood, "Just think, Tom, one of these 63Fs could buy a fleet of 250 Budd Conestogas!" Haywood playfully responded, "Yeah, and it would fly a hell of a lot better too." The occasion was graced by flight attendant representatives from various airlines that had placed orders including KLM, SAS, Seaboard, ONA, TIA, Air Canada and Viasa. Brigitte Schenk, fourth from the left, represented the Flying Tiger Line. The first Douglas DC-8-63, registered as N1503U, was painted in the manufacturer's livery with Douglas DC-8 Super 63 titles. It first flew on March 16 and, after 70 flights, was awarded type approval on June 10. This ship would later be delivered to KLM as PH-DEA and named Amerigo Vespucci.

Tom Haywood, second from the left, and Robert W. Prescott discussing the Jumbo Jet era with Brigitte Schenk and unknown executive.

Donald Douglas Jr at the podium introduces the DC-8-63 to the aviation industry. Donald Douglas Sr, pioneer aircraft developer and manufacturer, above centre, surrounded by airline executives including Robert W. Prescott in the back row.

Tom Haywood, left, and Robert W. Prescott in front of the first Douglas DC-8-63.

Delivery to the Royal Netherlands Air Force. A Lockheed F-104G Starfighter destined for the Royal Netherlands Air Force (Koninklijke Luchtmacht or KLu) is being carefully loaded into CL-44 N450T at Los Angeles Tiger base in April 1967, set for its journey to Twenthe air base. The KLu received a total of 138 Lockheed F-104G Starfighters between 1962 and 1967. While the majority of the KLu F-104Gs were built by Fokker, the particular F-104G depicted in the photograph was freshly manufactured by Lockheed in California and already featured the markings of the KLu. Notably, the fuselage serial numbers were temporarily concealed using tape.

Flying Tiger Air Services. Lockheed L-1049H Super Constellation N174W City of Naha of Flying Tiger Air Services (FTAS) in Bangkok on July 29, 1967. N174W was a very special Connie - it was the composite of two aircraft. The fuselage is from YC-121F 53-8158, one of two T34 turbine-powered prototypes of the YC-121F, while the wings, centre section, tail and engines are from L-1049G, YV-C-AME originally built and delivered in February 1956 to LAV - Linea Aeropostal Venezolana. Flying Tigers engineering and maintenance made two of these composite freighters in the same way between March and July 1963, the other being N173W. Both Connies were first used by the Flying Tiger Line from 1963 to 1966 before being transferred to business subsidiary Flying Tiger Air Services (FTAS) providing extensive all-cargo operations in the Far East, provision of spare parts, overhaul representation and assistance for overseas airlines. FTAS ended operations in December 1967 marking a final end of the Super Connie with Flying Tigers.

Jacques Guillem Collection

Swingtail leased. Spotted at Los Angeles International Airport in July 1967, the Canadair CL-44 swingtail with registration N229SW had been manufactured for Seaboard World Airlines and subsequently leased to the Flying Tiger Line on October 2, 1965.

New SFO terminal. Flying Tigers more than doubled the size of its Bay Area facility when it moved to a 32,000 square foot facility at San Francisco International Airport in November 1967. The move consolidated domestic sales and operations, maintenance, and international operations under one roof. To mark the event, model Romy Strauli came by to direct dock operations for a while. Getting the benefit of her directions (and presence) are ramp servicemen Ron Gibson (left) and Ben Woods (right).   Edwin Hoffman

Caledonian leasing. Spotted at San Francisco Airport is Boeing 707-399C N319F leased from Caledonian Airways from July 1967 till June 1968 in hybrid colours and was initially used on transatlantic group charters and tour charters in the United States. Interestingly, despite being directly leased by Caledonian and delivered from Seattle to Flying Tiger Line on July 13, 1967, this ship became the first 707 to enter service with Gatwick based Caledonian Airways (later British Caledonian) on June 8, 1968, as G-AVKA. Jacques Guillem Collection

A Tale of Kidnapping, Reunion, and Tragedy. The story of Jimmy, a baby Bengal tiger, started with his mysterious disappearance from the San Francisco Zoo in December 1967, leading to an intense search effort. Two days later, some hippies attempted to sell the stolen tiger cub to Ray Folsom's Reptile and Wild Animal Farm in Hermosa Beach, a coastal city in Los Angeles County. Unaware of the tiger's notoriety, Folsom bought Jimmy for $150. However, news broadcasts alerted Folsom about the tiger's kidnapping, prompting him to arrange its return. Flying Tigers were called upon to transport Jimmy back to the San Francisco Zoo. Escorted by Senior Captain Dick Rossi, Ray Folsom, and reporter Bill Moore, Jimmy's journey from Los Angeles to San Francisco was treated as a significant event. While it seemed like a joyful homecoming, tragedy struck a few days later when Jimmy choked on a piece of meat and died in the arms of his trainer.

Long Beach production. Spotted on the production line in Long Beach, the first Tiger Douglas DC-8-63F, with registration N779FT, was positioned between Swissair DC-8-62CF HB-IDH and United DC-8-61 N8086U. The second DC-8-63 for the Flying Tiger Line, N780FT, can be seen in the background.

Geoffrey Thomas

First Jumbo Jet. On a bustling day in April 1968, N779FT, stood amidst a vibrant scene at the Douglas Aircraft plant in Long Beach. Surrounding it were several other aircraft, including two DC-8-61s of United Air Lines also undergoing the final stages of completion. N779FT was delivered to the Flying Tiger Line on June 28, 1968, proudly adorned with eye-catching Jumbo Jet titles. However, the grandeur of these titles proved to be short-lived, adding to the aircraft's unique history.

Jumbo Jet

Aer Lingus leasing. Aer Lingus Boeing 707-348C, named "St. Brigid," was leased to the Flying Tiger Line under the registration N318F. This lease occurred between September 1966 to May 1967 and again from November 1967 to April 1968 when it reverted to its original registration, EI-ANO. It served to bridge the capacity gap while awaiting the arrival of the DC-8-63 in the fleet.

Andreas van Loon Collection

New flight training centre in operation. Opened in April 1968, the Flying Tiger Line's new flight training centre, though not aesthetically striking, was a model of modernity and sophistication in industrial facility design. The unpretentious structure, constructed by the Sheldon Appel Construction Company, cost less than $500,000 but housed cutting edge flight training equipment worth over $2 million. Under the direction of Captain Oakley Smith, the centre stood among the best in the airline industry, offering innovative training techniques to optimize student and instructor performance.

New DC-8-63F flight simulator. Pointing out features of the new DC-8-63F flight simulator in Flying Tiger Line's recently completed Flight Training Centre is Russ Kissinger, Manager of Simulator Engineering. Next to him, from left, are Captain Gene Taylor, Chief Flight Instructor, Tom Haywood, Supervisor of Flight Training, and Oakley Smith, Director of Flight Operations Training. Behind the four is the computer complex that controls the simulator. The state-of-the-art DC-8-63F flight simulator was built by the Link Division of General Precision Inc., representing an investment of $1.5 million. Notably, it was the sole unit of its kind installed on the entire West Coast.

Tiger in the cockpit. In May 1968, the Flying Tiger Line needed photographs of a live tiger in their settings for advertising purposes. They arranged to use Rijo, a 642-pound Siberian tiger from Ted Derby's Animal Kingdom, along with the expertise of renowned animal photographer Don Lewis. A Boeing 707 was positioned outside the maintenance facility for the photo shoot. However, their plans were foiled by rain, prompting them to come up with an innovative idea. Oakley Smith and Russ Kissinger, from the flight training and simulator engineering departments respectively, proposed using the new $1.5 million DC-8-63 flight simulator as an alternative backdrop for the tiger photoshoot. They successfully coaxed Rijo into the captain's seat of the simulator, capturing various shots of him interacting with fake packages, and posing for the camera. Pat Shelley, Ted Derby's wife, skilfully handled the tiger with affectionate coaxing.

MAC charter to Vietnam. Flying Tiger Line Boeing 707-349C N325F at Biên Hòa air base, northeast of Saigon, on 26 May 1968 on troop transport, supplies and equipment business for the Military Airlift Command. The MAC flights typically followed a planned routing from Travis or Norton Air Force Bases to Anchorage, Alaska (for crew change); then from Anchorage to Kadena Air Force Base, Okinawa (for crew change again); followed by the journey from Kadena to the designated destination in Vietnam and back to Kadena (for crew change); and finally from Kadena to McChord, Travis, or Norton Air Force Bases. John Bessette

Memorable encounter. On May 27, 1968, Leslie Ann Pfeifer, a flight attendant of Flying Tiger Line, found herself aboard a MAC Boeing 707-349C charter flight from Vietnam to Travis Air Force Base, California. During the flight, Leslie had a memorable encounter with a soldier who was part of a combat regiment in Vietnam. The soldier shared stories of his regiment's achievements, and he expressed immense pride in their accomplishments. Touched by their conversation, the soldier presented Leslie with his 2nd Cavalry Division insignia patch, creating a lasting memento of their encounter.

Leslie Ann Pfeifer

Summer Paris Orly spotting. During the summer of 1968, Flying Tiger Line's Boeing 707-349C N324F was sighted at Paris Orly. N324F completed its maiden flight from Renton on June 9, 1966, and was delivered to the Flying Tiger Line on June 21, 1966. Operated by Tiger crews, the aircraft was subleased to El Al from April to August 1968. During this period, the aircraft displayed El Al titles along with the inscription "on lease from Flying Tiger Line". The subsequent year, the aircraft featured in the original Airport movie adorned in Trans Global colours.

Jacques Guillem Collection

Layover in Paris. In the summer of 1968, Flying Tiger Line's Boeing 707-349C N325F was spotted parked at Paris–Le Bourget Airport. N325F made its first flight from Renton on February 2, 1967, and was delivered to Flying Tiger Line on February 6, 1967. The aircraft was leased from Boeing for a duration of two years. In addition to MAC flights, N325F was subleased to KLM from May to August 1967 and again from July to August 1968 for flights to the United States. Flown by Tiger crews, the aircraft was also subleased to El Al from September to December 1968, stepping in for N324F, which had been returned to Flying Tigers, and El Al's 707-458 4X-ATA, which was hijacked on July 23, 1968 by the Popular Front for the Liberation of Palestine and grounded in Algiers for five weeks. N325F concluded its service with the Flying Tiger Line in December 1968 and was subsequently acquired by Caledonian Airlines in January 1969.

Andreas van Loon Collection

Douglas DC-8-63CF first delivery. Seaboard World received the first DC-8-63CF aircraft, N8631, on June 21, 1968, promptly deploying it for MAC charter operations. Just a week later, Flying Tiger Line took delivery of its first DC-8-63CF aircraft, N779FT, on June 28, 1968, and a few days after, on July 1, the airline introduced the plane into its trans-Pacific military contract services. Flying Tiger had placed an order for 17 DC-8-63s, all of which could be converted for either passenger or cargo use.

Chairman of the Board of Directors Wayne M. Hoffman. At the delivery ceremony of the inaugural Tiger DC-63CF aircraft, Wayne M. Hoffman and Robert W. Prescott were prominent. Wayne M. Hoffman assumed the position of Chairman of the Board at the Flying Tiger Line in June 1967, succeeding Samuel B. Mosher, a key figure in the airline's founding alongside Prescott back in 1945. Hoffman had a background in the railroad and railways sector, and in 1962, he achieved a remarkable milestone by becoming the Executive Vice President of the New York Central Systems at the young age of 35, solidifying his status as one of the nation's youngest major transportation leaders.

Inaugural DC-8 to Vietnam. On July 6, 1968, the Flying Tiger Line inaugurated its first DC-8 Vietnam military charter flight to Saigon's Tan Son Nhut Airport. The aircraft, N779FT, configured as a combi, carried only 55,546 pounds of military cargo into Tan-Son-Nhut during its maiden flight. Despite the relatively light load, the freight was distributed over 15 pallets, prompting base commander Col. F. E. Peebles to remark, "You have just brought in the largest number of freight pallets ever flown into this base." The 17,197-mile flight, originating from Travis Air Force Base, San Francisco, to Tan-Son-Nhut, then to Tokyo and returning to Los Angeles, was completed in 31 hours and 50 minutes of actual flying time. LAX was reached 25 minutes ahead of the schedule set for the lengthy journey. As the first pallet of military supplies was unloaded, Chairman of the Board of Directors Wayne M. Hoffman (left) and Senior Vice President of Operations Edgar A. Pinke (right) oversaw the inaugural flight's aircraft offloading process, with armed guards surrounding the aircraft.

Charles Hillinger, Los Angeles Times

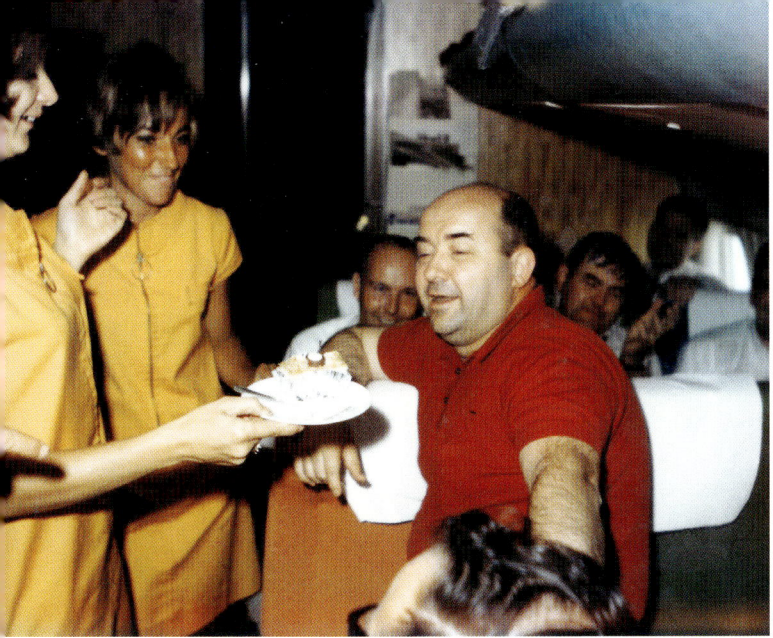

Marilyn Axelson Breen (on the left) and Pam Morgan were the two flight attendants on the last portion of the flight to Saigon's Tan Son Nhut Airport.

N779FT on the ground at Saigon's Tan Son Nhut Airport. The combi DC-8 had several passengers on board, including Flying Tiger Line executives Wayne M. Hoffman, Chairman of the Board, Don Morrissey, Director of Operations Services, and Ed Pinke, Senior Vice President of Operations. Reporter and photographer Charles Hillinger from the Los Angeles Times was also onboard the aircraft.

A group photo from the inaugural flight to Vietnam captures Marilyn Axelson Breen (on the left) and Pam Morgan (on the right) in the centre alongside the cockpit crew. Wayne Hoffman is positioned just behind Marilyn, with Ed Pinke to his left.

Flight Attendants Pam Morgan (left) and Marilyn Axelson Breen (right) enjoyed a jeep ride on the ramp of Tan Son Nhut Airport.

New markings. The Jumbo Jet appellation on Flying Tiger Line's first McDonnell Douglas DC-8-63F was discarded in August 1968 with the fourth aircraft, N782FT, as the carrier changed its markings. The heavy use of lettering along the fuselage tended to diminish the impression of length of the stretched aircraft and the whether Jumbo was appropriate for the DC-8-63F soon became questionable in view of even larger aircraft was also a factor (Flying Tigers announced its intention to purchase the Boeing 747 in March 1968). New markings included smaller Flying Tiger Line titles and a dark blue background field for red, white and blue circle T logo on the the vertical stabiliser. Above, Tigers' first DC-8-63AF N779FT at Hong Kong Kai Tak Airport in the new livery. The former Jumbo Jet title is still visible. Frank de Koster

Pole Cat farewell. Bidding the 707-349C Pole Cat a fond farewell, before joining Caledonian's fleet in Britain as G-AWTK, are her crew members on that memorable flight; from left to right; Chief Navigator Ernie Hickman; Captain Jack Martin, Director of Flying; and Second Officer Gene Olson. Besides the history-making Rockwell Polar Flight on November 16-17, 1965, N322F had a record breaking spree on her inaugural flight for the Tigers, under the co-captaincy of Jack Martin and J. P. Goldsmith. (Martin, incidentally, also flew her down to Burbank from the factory in Seattle on September 27, 1965.) She set her last speed and distance record in February, 1968, on a flight from Norton Air Force Base, California, to Yokota, Japan, with Captain B. V. Tharp in command, although there is a likelihood that her last flight for the Tigers, from Okinawa to Los Angeles in 10 hours and 10 minutes under Captain Ralph Hedden may also have set a new speed mark. Other Tiger captains who established point-to-point speed records with N322F are: John E. Long, J. J. Russell, R. L. Souers, R. P. Hedman, G. A. Myer, R. S. Allen, and D. E. Sanders. N322F served the Tigers well indeed, and continued to serve Caledonian Airways (later British Caledonian Airways in 1970) until 1977, when she was sold to TAAG Angola Airlines.

The largest single cantilevered structure. Tiger's maintenance hangar in Los Angeles was the largest single cantilevered structure west of Atlanta. It encompassed 162,517 square feet of floor space, including upstairs shops and offices, and was spacious enough to accommodate three DC-8-63s simultaneously. Inside the hangar, from left to right, are DC-8-63 N625FT, leased by CP Air from July to December 1968; DC-8-63AF N786FT, delivered in December 1968; and DC-8-63CF N781FT, the third DC-8 delivered to the Flying Tine Line in July 1968.

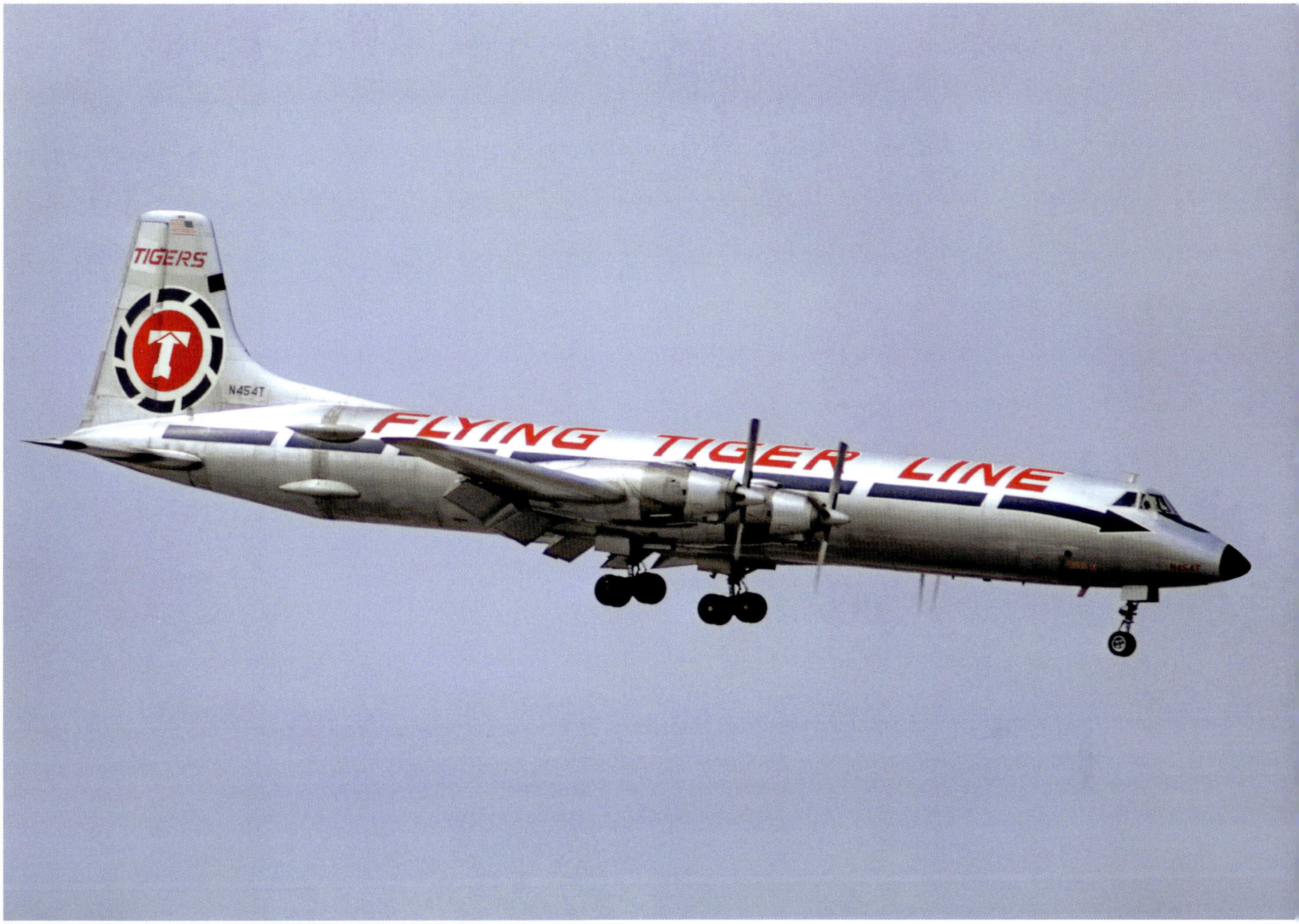

Coming in to land. Flying Tiger Line's Canadair CL-44 N454T was observed on final approach to Los Angeles International Airport in February 1969. Originally built for Tiger, it took its inaugural flight on November 28, 1961, and was delivered on January 25, 1962.   Jacques Guillem Collection

Tiger 707 in a blockbuster movie. The Tiger Boeing 707-349C N324F played a prominent role in the classic movie Airport, a disaster motion picture released in 1970. It was one of seven 707s operated by Flying Tigers from 1965 to 1969 and was leased by Universal Pictures for the film's production between January 28 and March 8, 1969. During filming, N324F was made to look like a fictional Trans Global Airlines (TGA) aircraft with an El Al cheatline from a previous lease over its bare metal finish. The plot of the movie depicted the airliner suffering from explosive decompression caused by a bomb blast in the rear lavatory, forcing a dramatic landing. After its appearance in the movie, the aircraft returned to Los Angeles. As the Flying Tigers was transitioning to the DC-8, Boeing sold N324F to Aer Lingus in April 1969. Subsequently, the aircraft had a varied career, being leased to several carriers, including Qantas, British Caledonian, and Zambia Airways. Unfortunately, the plane met a tragic end on March 21, 1989, during a high-speed approach near São Paulo, Brazil. It crashed in a heavily populated suburb, resulting in the deaths of three crew members and 22 people on the ground, with over 200 others injured. Above, N324F on March 8, 1969 - back in Tigers' Los Angeles base.

Ted Gibson, via John Wegg

Former Tiger CL-44 in body-building exercise. In May 1969, the Conroy Aircraft Corporation, based in Santa Barbara, California, embarked on a significant conversion project. They transformed former Tiger CL-44 N447T aircraft to serve as a carrier for large jet engines, oil drilling rigs, prefabricated housing, and other equipment and supplies to support oil exploration on the North Slope of Alaska. The conversion process involved removing the upper half of the fuselage, which weighed nearly 5,000 pounds and measured 84 feet in length. To expand the maximum interior diameter of the aircraft to 14 feet nine inches, skilled workers utilised prefabricated frames and stringers. This ingenious modification increased the plane's capacity by an impressive 100 per cent. The result was a new CL-44 capable of carrying a payload of 30 tons or more. Conroy had plans to modify several CL-44s to various dimensions, and a firm order was placed for a second aircraft but N446T, its source airframe, crashed before delivery on May 1, 1969. The surviving example, initially named Skymonster by Transmeridian Air Cargo in 1970, later known as Bahamas Trader, underwent multiple changes in ownership and registrations. British Cargo Airlines acquired it in 1978, followed by HeavyLift Cargo Airlines in 1982 under the Irish registration EI-BND, and leased to Buffalo Airways and Azerbaijan Airlines in the 1990s. In 1999, it was placed in storage in the US before being flown to Bournemouth International Airport, UK, where it faced the possibility of scrapping. As of February 2024, the aircraft was still intact at Bournemouth waiting an uncertain future.

Vietnam crew corner

In February 1969, on a Flying Tiger Line 707 flight to Vietnam, Flight Attendants Josie Sager Gibson (on the left) and Susie Rodriguez (on the right) laughed and talked with GIs aboard the flight. Jerry Plank, on Josie's left, corresponded with her throughout his tour in Vietnam.

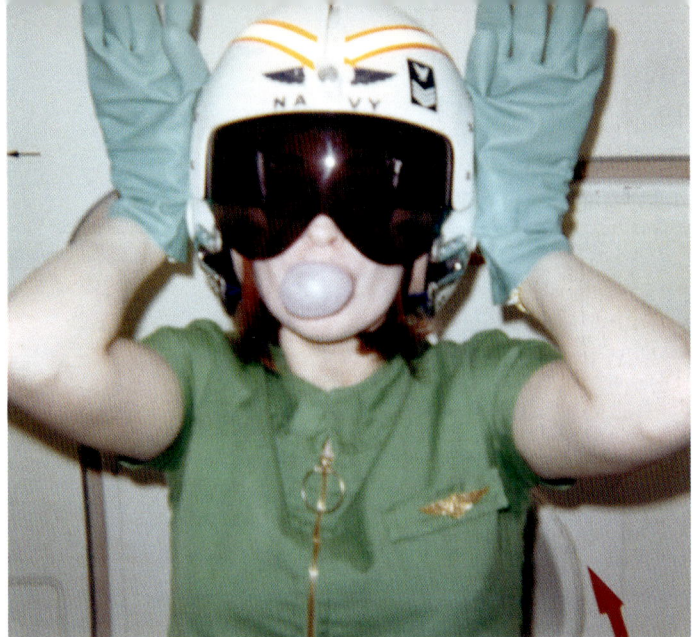

In March 1969, Flight Attendant Ann Price Montgomery infused humor and laughter into a flight as she worked in the aft galley on a DC-8.

Flight Attendants Maureen Amiot Thomas, standing, and Holly Comstock Lefkowitz, seated, enjoyed a jeep ride on the beach of Cam Ranh Bay in March 1969.

Flight Attendant Leslie Laird Pfeifer pictured with Captain Robert E. "Bob" Clutter (on the left) and First Officer John Hess somewhere in Vietnam in July 1969. (Hess served as the Second Officer during that period.)   Photos by Josie Sager Gibson

Tigers' Former Stewardesses in Palm Springs Reunion. Sixteen former Flying Tiger Line stewardesses, who had previously delivered outstanding service to passengers aboard Tiger charter flights, came together for their annual Clipped Wings reunion in July 1969. Prior to the election of new officers, a special dinner was held to honor Bob and Anne Marie Prescott. These dedicated individuals maintained their connection with Tiger-related endeavors, actively contributing to the construction of the Peter Prescott Memorial Hospital in Taipei, Taiwan, as well as raising funds for both Crippled Children's and Veterans' Hospitals. From left to right are Fran Drew Whitesides, Michelle McKenzie, Robert W. Prescott and June Drew Ebensteiner, twin sister of Fran.

First scheduled all-Cargo service to Orient. On August 12, 1969, Flying Tiger Line initiated its inaugural transpacific flight using the DC-8-63F aircraft with the registration N785FT. The journey commenced in San Francisco and included a stop in Seattle to accommodate additional mail and cargo. From there, it continued to Okinawa and Saigon via Cold Bay in Alaska, carrying a substantial load of 89,300 pounds of military mail and cargo. This flight represented a long-anticipated milestone, the culmination of extensive efforts to secure Route 163, renowned as one of the most profitable air cargo routes worldwide. At the time, the San Francisco-Seattle to Okinawa and Saigon route was served by only two carriers: Northwest Orient, offering service to Okinawa, and Pan American, connecting to Saigon. It is important to mention that Flying Tiger Line brought extensive experience to this region, with a track record of having flown over 400 million miles in contract and charter services there.

Tiger Stewardess Robin Burkey helped Bob Prescott to affix an oversized airmail stamp on the first pallet of mail out of Seattle on Tiger's inaugural flight

Bob Prescott, stewardess Marcy Massie and Colonel Lester R. Ferris, Travis Air Force Base. In the background is new Super 63 N785FT which was utilised for the inaugural transpacific Route 163 flight. Regrettably, less than a year later, on final approach to Naha Air Force Base on Okinawa Island, N785FT was tragically lost in an accident, resulting in the loss of all four on board.

With the help of military officers, San Francisco's Mayor Joseph Alioto (middle right) helped Board Chairman Wayne Hoffman load the first mail aboard the historic Tiger flight while Robert W. Prescott watched from the plane with stewardess Judy Vaughn.

Officials gathered for the inaugural Route 163 ceremonies in San Francisco, where the airline was bestowed with a symbolic key to the city. In the photograph, from left to right, Tiger Stewardesses Betty Carver, Penny Bowles, Robin Burkey, Marcy Massie, and Judy Vaughn can be seen attending the event, listening to the officials and Robert W. Prescott as he expressed his gratitude for the opportunity to extend Tiger's domestic system overseas to cater to the trade areas of the Orient. "More than 10 years ago, we filed our first application for this route and since then it has gone through two full Civil Aeronautics Board hearings and the offices of four presidents," Prescott remarked.

Vano Wells Fagliano

Inaugural flight to Tokyo. With the introduction of the new Transpacific Route 163, which included stops in San Francisco, Seattle, and, weather permitting, Cold Bay, Alaska, Haneda Airport in Tokyo assumed a pivotal role once Japan confirmed the vital uplift rights on September 2, 1969. On September 15, the first scheduled international flight for the Flying Tiger Line landed at Haneda. Prior to this development, Haneda primarily served as a diversion point for military charter flights into Yokota, as the airport was operating at full capacity. It remained Tokyo's primary international airport until 1978, when Narita Airport opened. The inaugural flight to Tokyo departed from Los Angeles on September 14, with Captain Tom Mitchell at the helm (captured in the photo shaking hands with his 10-year-old son, Tom, Jr.) First Officer Dick Hill and Flight Engineer Don Singer were also on board, and Navigator Chuck Bellows joined the crew in San Francisco. There was a crew change in Cold Bay for the final leg of the journey to Tokyo. Photography, Inc.

Last Tiger CL-44 revenue flight. On a Sunday afternoon, September 14, 1969, the last CL-44 revenue flight for Flying Tigers pulled up in the shadow of a gleaming DC-8 being groomed for the inaugural fight to Tokyo. The CL-44 seemed small as it taxied into position on the loading ramp, the tail slowly opened, and fork lifts began unloading the 34,606 pounds of cargo from the east coast. The crew of the last flight was Captain Ron Hall, (right), First Officer Monty Lewis, both of Newark, with Flight Engineer Dave Cawthorne of Los Angeles. Good flight, the crew agreed, good plane, no problems. Quietly the "little" CL-44 retired.

Shark-toothed DC-8 Tiger. The delivery of the Tiger's seventeenth and final DC-8 on October 3, 1969 stirred excitement and imagination at the Long Beach factory, sporting a shark-toothed smile, a playful arrangement was orchestrated by Ken Hale, Tigers' senior representative at McDonnell Douglas, in collaboration with Douglas officials. Hale revealed, "One afternoon, we were discussing the fact that business had become so darned serious that there was never time for laughs anymore. It crossed my mind we should add the shark's teeth to our final DC-8 delivery as a surprise for the old timers." The famous shark's teeth, worn by the original Flying Tigers in the Chinese civil war, were applied to the DC-8 using washable colors for easy removal. "I kept it quiet 'til the last minute," Hale confessed. "I was afraid somebody would throw a wrench in my plans." Before the aircraft was ferried to Los Angeles, a team of Douglas and Flying Tigers officials gathered for a photo next to N796FT, the final Tiger DC-8-63CF. The individuals, from left to right, included two probable Douglas staff; two unknown; Edgar E. Pinke, Senior VP operations; unknown; Arthur F. "Art" Seymour, VP flight operations; John T. White, director of flying; George Maruyama, Manager quality control; Joe Palotti, Manager of maintenance contracts, and two probable Douglas staff.

A captivating aerial perspective captures N796FT, the seventeenth DC-8-63CF of Flying Tiger Line, adorned with the distinctive colors of shark's teeth, a signature of the fighter planes in the original AVG that flew in combat in China.

Come fly with us! In September 1969, a group of six Flying Tiger flight attendants in Asia. From left to right: unidentified, Nicole DeGregario, Lynne R. Rayner, Patty Manley, Carolyn Gonet, and unidentified, posing on the stairs of a DC-8-63.   Lynne R. Rayner

Hands-on. In October 1969, a maintenance crew was engaged in an engine change for a DC-8-63. The JT3D-3 engine cowling had been taken off. Unlike the usual "nose in" arrangement, the DC-8-63 was parked "tail in" in the vast Flying Tiger maintenance hangar in Los Angeles. The JT3D-3 engine was slated for overhaul.   Laurie Fish

Hong Kong Tiger. In December 1969, brand-new DC-8-63CF N779FT, the first stretched DC-8 for the Flying Tiger Line, was present at Hong Kong Kai Tak International Airport. Notably, the original (though still visible) Flying Tiger Jumbo Jet lettering had been replaced with smaller Flying Tiger Line titles.

Leonard Nadel

Coming in to land. Douglas DC-8-63CF N792FT on approach to runway 13 at Hong Kong Kai Tak Airport.

Charter from Tokyo to Los Angeles. Valerie Pestano, the charter coordinator for Flying Tiger Line, oversaw the delivery of an 80,000-pound shipment of Craig products, which included portable cassette player recorders and AM/FM stereo tuners, to Hal Kanngiesser, the sales administrator at Craig. In December 1969, Craig chartered four DC-8 flights from its factory sources in Japan to meet the high demand during the US holiday season. These flights originated in Tokyo Haneda and arrived in Los Angeles.

Airliners of hope. The "Freedom Bird" held special significance for U.S. military personnel during the Vietnam War, as this was the aircraft that would return them home at the end of their tours. Throughout the conflict, troops were transported to and from Vietnam on commercial airliners contracted by the U.S. Air Force Military Airlift Command (MAC) and operated by civilian crews and flight attendants. Various carriers were involved including American Airlines, Continental Airlines, Flying Tiger Line, Overseas National, Seaboard World Airlines, Trans International, Saturn Airways and United Airlines. DC-8-63 N795FT was photographed at Cam Ranh Bay, Vietnam in March 1970 as military personnel boarded the aircraft. Laurie V. Fish

Going home. In March 1970, military personnel were photographed boarding a DC-8-63 bound for the United States at Cam Ranh Bay, South Vietnam. In the background, a TIA - Trans International Airlines DC-8-63 MAC flight was seen ready to depart.

Laurie V. Fish

Moral support. Throughout the war, thousands of flights criss-crossed the Pacific Ocean, each one representing a deeply emotional journey for military personnel and the young women who served as flight attendants. Accompanying anxious servicemen into war zones, these women provided valuable moral support. During return flights, they offered compassion to exhausted soldiers, elated to be going home but still traumatised by their wartime experiences. The flight attendants gained a unique perspective on their country at war and despite their crucial role, their contributions have remained largely unacknowledged beyond the veteran community. From left to right: Sandy Ferguson, Mary O'Hearn, Myra Singer, unknown, unknown and Lora Di Renzo waited beside the stairs as troops boarded the Tiger flight at Cam Ranh Bay in March 1970.   Laurie V. Fish

Da Nang, South Vietnam. Having arrived from Cam Ranh Bay in March 1970 during a Military Airlift Command operation, a Tiger crew posed proudly in front of their DC-8 on the ramp in Da Nang before their onward flight to Tokyo. From left to right: unknown ground staff, Captain George "Frank" Morrow, Flight Engineer Ralph E. Smith and First Officer Lenny Renda. Laurie V. Fish

Vital contribution. From April 1969 to March 1970, Tigers completed more than 400 passenger missions flying DC-8-63s in and out of Vietnam transporting approximately 180,000 military personnel on behalf of the Military Airlift Command. Moreover, between August 1969 and March 1970, the airline delivered over 15 million pounds of military mail to the four Tiger stations in Vietnam that were run by Flying Tiger Line's Operations Services. These were strategically located in Tan Son Nhut, Bien Hoa, Cam Ranh Bay and Da Nang. This remarkable commitment underscores the vital role Tigers played during this challenging period. Here military personnel were seen boarding N795FT at Cam Ranh Bay in March 1970. Laurie V. Fish

Maintaining high standards. Members of the senior staff of instructors and check stewardesses were photographed at McChord Air Force Base, Washington. Standing in the back row: Betty Carver, Marilyn Axelson, Verla Massie and Nancy Brennan. In the front row: Bonnie Colton, Margaret Hough, who served as the Chief Flight Attendant and Brenda J. Brown, the Assistant Chief Flight Attendant. This dedicated team played a critical role in upholding the high standards of service and safety for Flying Tiger Line passenger operations. Richards Studio, Tacoma

Before and after. Flying Tiger DC-8-63AF N790FT standing by in Da Nang with four 40k loaders lined up to deal with numerous incoming pallets. The equipment used in Cam Ranh Bay was very long and unwieldy so it was replaced with two new Cochran loaders specially designed for the task. These were disassembled in Los Angeles during May 1970, shipped to Vietnam and reassembled on site. Working in searing heat, Ralph Blum, a motor pool mechanic from Los Angeles, Tony Grajiola, the maintenance representative in Cold Bay, R. E. "Scotty" Scott, a line mechanic, and Bill Crysell, a senior maintenance representative in the Far East, demonstrated their unwavering "Can Do" spirit during the reassembly process in Cam Ranh Bay and Da Nang. USAF

Before and after. A side-by-side comparison reveals the evolution of Tiger cabin crew uniforms. On the left, Robin Burkey and Marcey Massie bid adieu to the red wool A-shape dresses they had been wearing, while on the right, Kathleen Skrha showcases the new four-piece navy blue ensemble, paired with navy blue leather accessories, representing a more versatile and contemporary look.

Richards Studio, Tacoma

Nostalgic gathering. Flying Tiger Line founder Robert W. Prescott surrounded by past flight attendants during a weekend in Palm Springs in July 1970 in appreciation of the carrier's Far East runs. Taken at the Hungry Tiger restaurant, from left to right, the back row comprises unknown former Tiger stewardess, Donalda Towne, Bobbie Fowles Van Norstrand, Pamela Trott Hunter, unknown, Patti Bliss, unknown, Inga Mitchell and another unknown stewardess. In the front row: unknown, Billie Welch Garrick, Del Florzak Noland, Ann Ludwig, Trudy Mareschal Bogart, Maggee Thompson, Michelle McKenzie, Robert W. Prescott, two more unknown, Jan Marshall and another unknown former stewardess round out the front row. *Pamela Trott Hunter Collection*

Silver Anniversary. On July 14, 1970, the Flying Tiger Line celebrated its 25th anniversary with an elegant dinner at the Beverly Wilshire Hotel in Los Angeles, California. Radio and television personality Art Linkletter served as Master of Ceremonies for the evening, the highlight of which was a "This is Your Life" style tribute to Robert W. "Bob" Prescott. Bob's family, friends, partners and business associates gathered to share stories and laughter as they recounted Bob's journey to success. One amusing anecdote involved Frances Drew, who arrived on stage wearing her original Flying Tiger cabin crew uniform and carrying a 'honey bucket' (or dry toilet). Having arrived in Honolulu on her first overseas trip she recalled how the captain told her she would have to empty the honey bucket. Puzzled, she asked, "Where?" To her surprise, he replied, "In the terminal!" Fran carried the bucket into the terminal, where an officer approached her, inquiring, "What are you doing?" she responded with a chuckle, "I'm looking for a place to empty this."

Devastating loss. On July 27, 1970, tragedy struck when Tiger DC-8-63AF N785FT crashed into the water near the north end of the runway overrun at Naha Air Base in Okinawa, with the loss of all four crew members. The aircraft, en route from Tokyo to Hong Kong on a cargo flight, fell short while conducting a Precision Approach Radar landing. Captain Cleo M. Treft, First Officer Robert E. Foley, Second Officer William A. George, and Navigator Walter M. Robert survived the impact of the crash but drowned in the aircraft due to the tide rising rapidly before emergency ground personnel could save them. N785FT, having accumulated 6,047.2 flight hours, was the only loss of a DC-8 in the airline's history. The probable cause was attributed to "an unarrested rate of descent" as the crew sought visual contact during adverse weather conditions. Photographs depicting the crash site and recovered parts played a crucial role in the investigation.

Far East tour. Robert W. Prescott (second from left), President of the Flying Tiger Line, and his daughter, French, flew into Tokyo via Pan American on September 18, 1970 to host celebrations marking the Tigers' 25th anniversary. Similar tributes also took place in Taiwan and Korea. Vice President Far East George A. Zettler (on the right), Mrs Rosemary Zettler and Richard C. Schaklee (left), general terminal manager - Japan, were on hand at the new passenger arrival terminal of Tokyo Haneda to greet the Prescotts.
Lee and Williams Company

Picture perfect. Captain Robert "Bob" Martin took this striking image of a Tiger DC-8-63F taking off from Cold Bay circa November 1970. Pictured against a dramatic Alaskan sky, this shot captures the moment the sun broke through, casting its warm glow on the aircraft as it headed out to Tokyo. Bob Martin, a keen amateur photographer, carried his camera with him all the time and shared his work with the company. Robert "Bob" Martin

Unsung heroines. The Flying Tiger Line provided six flight attendants for each DC-8-63 military passenger mission, the teams being specially dedicated to the wellbeing of the 219 passengers. Led by Chief Flight Attendant Margaret "Marge" Hough, these women underwent exhaustive training, mastering emergency procedures, first aid and equipment operation. Between April 1969 and December 1970 their responsibilities were extended to over 200,000 troops being transported to and from Vietnam. Their role demanded a blend of compassion, distraction and sisterly support as they tended to the needs of military personnel and this led to them forming a tight-knit camaraderie within the McChord Air Force Base community. Despite daunting schedules and significant challenges, the flight attendants embraced their identity as Tigers and took great pride in serving those facing testing times.

Marge Hough, Chief Flight Attendant (since 1963) logs in a colleague on the board at McChord Air Force Base. The duty status and whereabouts of every flight attendant was noted in coloured crayon on several white plastic boards. In total 130 flight attendants were on active duty in December 1970.

Shirley Keller photographed in the galley of N795FT prior to departure from McChord Air Force Base.

Kathe Anne Michalek posed with passengers on board DC-8-63 N795FT at McChord Air Force Base. The men were flying into the unknown, their last contact with a world of happier days would be the compassionate care of the Tiger attendants.

Crew corner

From left to right, Navigator Al La Forge, Captain Robert Gilbert and Second Officer Kenneth Boyd checked in for a DC-8-63 passenger flight out of McChord Air Force Base, Washington.

First Officer Hank Germain, left, with Captain Bill Towner, Assistant Chief Pilot, Newark.

First Officer Karl Krout runs down a check list prior to take-off from Seattle.

Second Officer Frank McGreal performs a pre-flight check.

In August 1971, First Officer Peter A. Okicich, left, and Captain Rowan N. Neff checked in for their flight from San Francisco.

In April 1971, Senior Captain Robert L "Bob" Blanck was in command of a DC-8-63F. Following his initial hiring in 1946, he was later laid off and did not resume flying until February 1951, when he rejoined Flying Tigers. Laurie V. Fish

DC-8 Navigator John R. Newman in April 1971. Laurie V. Fish

First Officer Ron Smith in April 1971. Laurie V. Fish

New wings at McChord. Twenty-eight new Tiger flight attendants received their diplomas and their wings (pinned to blue and white uniforms) in July 1971 at McChord AFB in Washington. This picture shows twenty-four of them. From left to right, kneeling - front row: Rhonda Martin, Brenda Wallace, Laura Harrington, Valerie Lindberg, Joyce Dong, Rose Walters, Helen Harris, Janet Cooper and Gwendolyn Ray. Behind: between both rows, is Lynn Westfall. Standing - back row, from left: Esperanza Davis, Jutta Cousineau, Alice Mendez, Edith McGeough, Lilly Ishii, Kristina Mick, Janet Holt, Gertrude Altig, Laura Vines, Gladine Williams, Harriet Williams, Alexandra Plommer, Vickie Baughn, Mary Harvey. Both Janet Preston, JoAnn Taylor, Betty Torres and Beverly Lavert are not shown.

Final finesse. A ground crew member leaning out of the cockpit window to remove marks from the Tiger DC-8-63F's windscreen.

Catering check in Vietnam. In August 1971, upon arriving from Tokyo, Bill Corp, the operating supervisor, boarded the DC-8 in Cam Ranh Bay to review the list of food supplies with Tiger stewardess Marjorie Evans. The aircraft is poised to transport weary but relieved servicemen on their journey to McChord Air Force Base, a 14-hour flight from Vietnam via Tokyo.

Crew corner

From left to right, Captain Donald E. Riggs, along with crewmembers Larry D. Barrow and Howard L. Harder, were photographed in Los Angeles on September 15, 1971. Behind them, DC-8-63AF N788FT was being loaded for a horse transport charter for the Royal Canadian Mounted Police.   Laurie Fish

Captain Tom T. Grider, First Officer Paul G. "Pat" Patterson, and Second Officer Arthur C. Guy, a career flight engineer, were all smiles aboard DC-8-63CF N796FT in San Francisco on August 17, 1971.   Laurie Fish

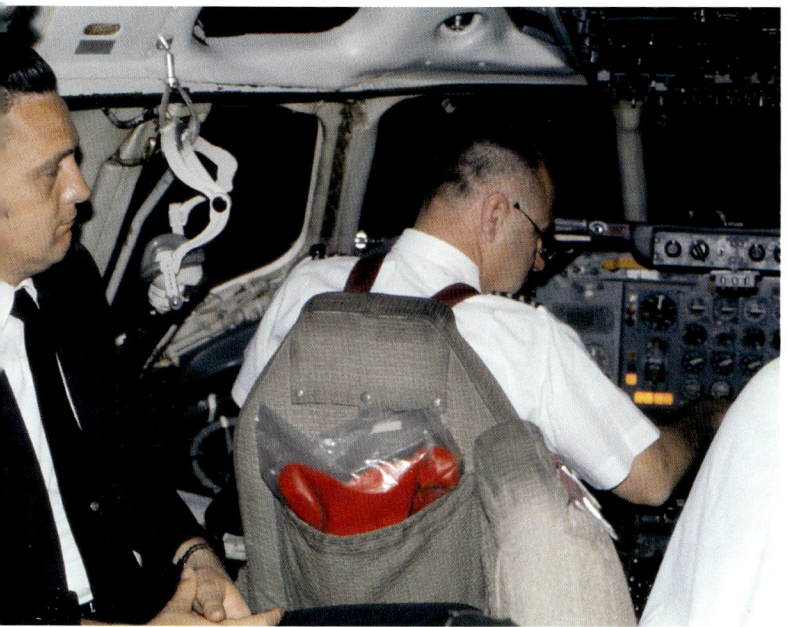

Captain Howell G. "Rick" Rickman observed the preparation of the crew from the DC-8 jumpseat in April 1971.

In 1971, DC-8-63 crews included navigators positioned next to the radio rack. Seated at a table with a control panel, navigators had several indicators such as drift angle, air speed and a LORAN screen. Prior to the installatiion of INS equipment, their role extended beyond verifying position to include updating charts and ensuring flights followed planned routes

Oil equipment challenge. Late in October 1971, Jim Morrisroe, Tigers' sales representative in Dallas, oversaw a difficult shipment of oil-drilling equipment via DC-8-63F from Los Angeles to New York Kennedy, for its eventual destination, Stavangar, Norway, aboard SAS. The 51,211lbs of gear took up ten pallet positions and included two giant shafts, each measuring 235 in length by 35 and 32 inches. Each shaft weighed 8,820lbs. McLean Cargo Specialists of Houston were acting as agents for VETCO, one of the world's leading suppliers of drilling, completion and production equipment for on- and offshore oil and gas fields. The loading required a great deal of skill on the part of the Los Angeles ramp personnel. Brett Fish

Hi-Tiger groundbreaking. On April 11, 1972, a tractor rumbled into position in the east parking lot outside the Flying Tiger Corporation headquarters in Los Angeles and nonchalantly broke ground on the blacktop surface. Shortly after, the "upstairs team", along with esteemed guests and airport officials gathered for the momentous occasion. On the left, Clifton Moore, the general manager of the Department of Airports, joined Robert W. Prescott and C. Lemoine Blanchard, the Airport Commission president, while Wayne Hoffman wielded a specially designed four-handled shovel. During the lunch-break, Tigers looked on with wide grins, adding to the festive atmosphere. This marked the second groundbreaking ceremony for a Tiger facility at the airport in seven years. The "old" two-storey general office building, completed in February 1966, had become too small to accommodate the company's rapid growth. Months of construction lay ahead for what would become Hi-Tiger, the new world headquarters. This ten-storey corporate HQ would become the second tallest structure at the airport after the control tower. John Tymczyszyn Archives

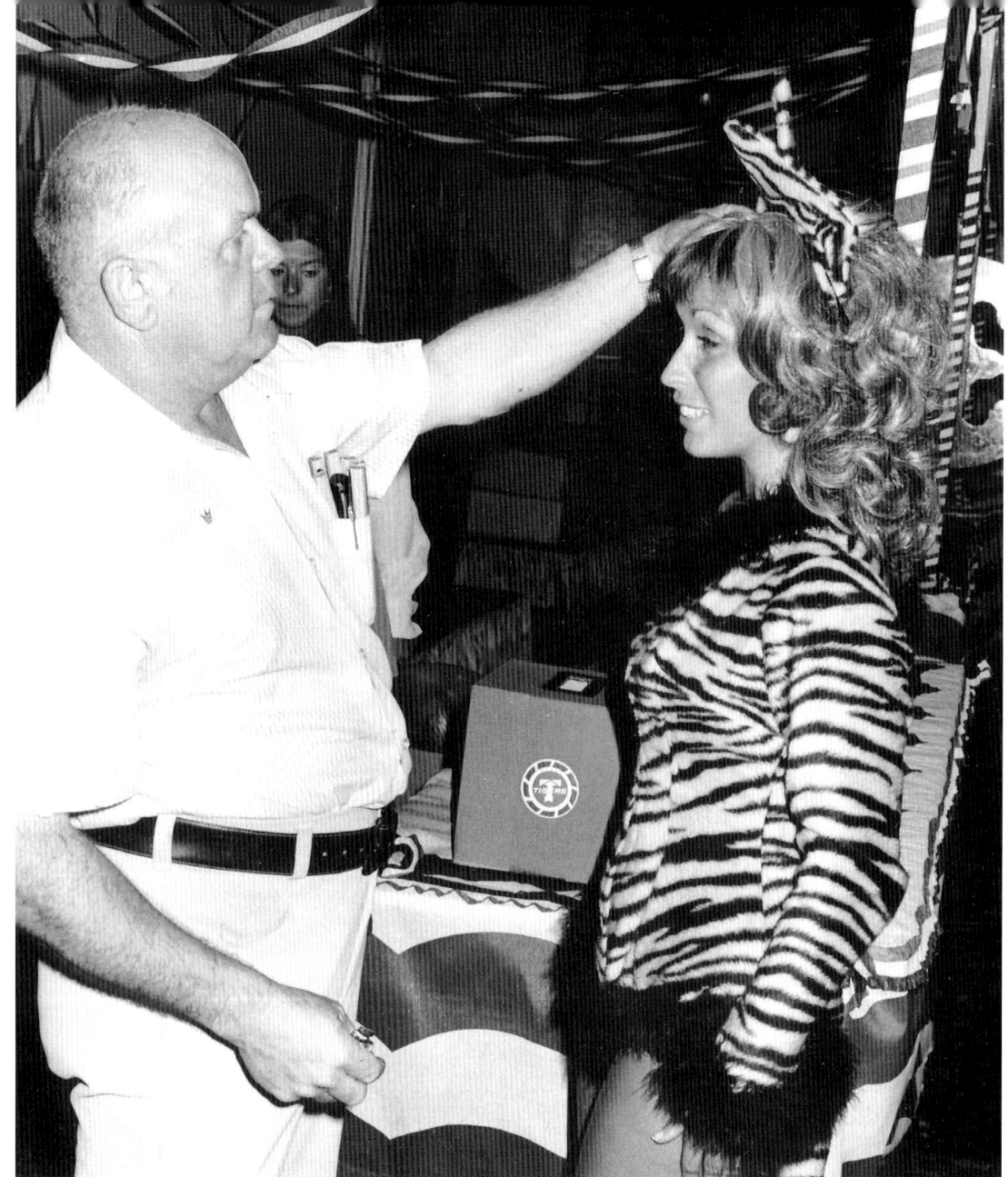

Interline party. Alfred J. "Al" Cormier straightened Sandy Amato's tiger ears during an interline party sponsored by Flying Tiger in Los Angeles in July 1972. Cormier began in April 1951 as a junior structure mechanic and progressed through various maintenance roles, including Arctic Dewline duty. Recognised for his exceptional commitment, Cormier became the go-to person for special tasks, earning him the titles of Special Projects Foreman and later Manager of Special Projects. He handled diverse responsibilities, from company projects to public relations and salvage sales. Day and night, Cormier, rarely seen without an unlit cigar, embodied the Flying Tigers' can-do spirit, from collecting gifts and donations for orphanages in Vietnam and Korea to setting up Christmas events, retirement parties and employee picnics.

Anchorage Departure. Delivered on March 3, 1969, N792FT marked the sixth addition to the fleet of stretched DC-8s operated by Flying Tiger Line. The photograph captures the moment the aircraft's nosewheel lifted off the runway in Anchorage. John Wegg

New wings for the Tiger family. North American Car became an integral part of the Flying Tiger Corporation family, known for having "its fleet on the ground," and specialising in railroad equipment leasing. With the acquisition of National Equipment Rental in September 1971, NER's subsidiary, National Aircraft Leasing (NAL), became yet another arm of the Flying Tiger Corp. NAL, dedicated to leasing turboprop and jet aircraft to airlines and corporations worldwide, expanded its fleet from 17 to 29 turboprop and turbojet aircraft, including a number of British-built One-Elevens, which became the epitome of executive jet aircraft. These BAC 1-11-401AK One-Elevens were formerly used by American Airlines. Dee Howard & Company of San Antonio designed the interior, which boasted two private staterooms, a lounge, bar, full galley and an office space complete with executive desk and sky-phone. The first NAL 1-11, N111NA c/n 055, proudly displaying the Tiger T on its tail and served as a demonstrator for the Flying Tiger Corporation. Similarly, N111NA, N5036 (c/n 078) also wore the Tiger T tail logo.

Spreading its wings. In July 1973, the Flying Tiger Line added UTA - Union de Transports Aériens - to its portfolio to undertake maintenance at the Los Angeles hangar. UTA had been formed from the merger of the Union Aéromaritime de Transport (UAT) and Transports Aériens Intercontinentaux (TAI). It was TAI that had pioneered French independent airline routes through the South Pacific, particularly to the French overseas territories of Tahiti and New Caledonia. The DC-8-62s, which FTL maintained, flew in a pattern that included Nouméa, Auckland and Tahiti. The world tour route from Paris-Karachi-Saigon-Singapore into Los Angeles was operated by the new DC-10-30s, and Air France continued the route from Los Angeles to Paris. At the time, this was the longest single carrier route in the world covering approximately 20,000 miles. Due to the remoteness of the DC-8 part of the UTA operation from Paris, Tigers effectively acted as UTA's line maintenance "programme manager" in the Pacific area in conjunction with UTA maintenance staff in Papeete.

New Vital II simulator. In December 1973, after months of preparation, the Samuel B. Mosher Flight Training Center unveiled a new McDonnell Douglas Vital II visual simulation system on its DC-8-63. What resembled four TV sets straddled the nose of the DC-8 flight simulator and showed computer-generated lights from signals provided by the flight simulator's own computers. As trainee crew members 'steered' the DC-8 simulator towards their destination airport, runway and city lights appeared at the cockpit's front and side windows, mirroring an actual night approach. The effect was also three dimensional, with lights changing in size, position and seemingly in distance as they navigated through circling approaches, landings and takeoffs. It was so realistic that some individuals were known to experience airsickness. The Vital II system enabled Tigers to transfer nine training manoeuvres that previously required aircraft checkrides to the simulator.

Tigers and Anna Chennault. Tiger Board Chairman Wayne M. Hoffman and President Robert W. Prescott met with Anna Chennault, Vice-President International Affairs at their Los Angeles home base. Anna, born Chen Xiangmei in 1923, lived a rich and tumultuous life. As a war correspondent during World War II, she secured an interview with Claire Lee Chennault, leader of the Flying Tigers, and married him in 1947. The couple supported nationalist forces in China but eventually retreated to Taiwan. A staunch anti-communist, Anna continued lobbying in Washington. In 1968, she played a covert role during the Vietnam peace talks, aiding Nixon's election. Despite her efforts, Nixon denied her a position and she fell out of favour when he pursued détente with the communists. She died in spring 2018 aged 94.

Flying high. In April 1974, the Flying Tiger Line ran charter flights to take trapeze artists from Spain's famous Los Muchachos Circus from Caracas Maiquetia Airport to Tokyo Haneda for a six-month tour of Japan under a contract with the Nippon Educational Television Company. The Circus was a self-supporting organisation for underpriviledged boys founded seven years previously by Father Jesus Silva. The Tigers' new commitment with the Circus was a three-ring event. In the main ring, Flight Attendants Diane Hernandez, Grace Janosko, Brigitte Sprenger and Marilyn Axelrod-Breen boarded 85 passengers, most of them daring young men of the flying trapeze. Operations Services Catering Supervisor Jim Brodie ensured he had enough food cooked up for this mini army, while up front, Captain H. P. Watkins, First Officer Dwight Small and Flight Engineer Bob Zopfi reviewed flight plans. In another ring, Senior Ops Supervisor Gene Ford of Travis co-ordinated trunks containing valuable and elaborate circus costumes. In the third ring, Bob Murty of Murty Brothers oversaw the loading of a circus pony and seven magnificent performing horses. "Tachikawa" Ted Chikowski, JFK lead mechanic, checked the aircraft for departure as Charter Sales' Ken Roe collected manifests. Pictured are the 85 members of Los Muchachos Circus on arrival in Tokyo. They were scheduled to appear in Hiroshima, Fukuoka, Nagoya, Hokkaido and 12 other cities in Japan. Members of the Imperial family were in the audience on opening night.

A whale of a trip. On April 17, 1974, a 19-foot-long, 5,000lb killer whale named Shamu (known as Kilroy in his private life) was transported via Flying Tigers DC-8-63CF N792FT from San Diego's Lindbergh Field to Cleveland's Hopkins Airport. For the occasion, the aircraft's nose section was adorned with "Sea World Flying Tiger Orc-Ark" titles after Orcinus-Orca, the generic name for the killer whale and a nod to Noah's Ark. Shamu-Kilroy was just one of several Sea World performers scheduled to fly to Cleveland for their summer performances at Sea World's Midwest Park. The 66,000lb cargo of sea creatures included a 3,500lb elephant seal, 14 California sea lions, three harbor seals, 10 bottlenose dolphins, four penguins, tropical fish, a dog and a piano-playing duck.

Tigers say "hi" to Hi Tiger. On June 8, 1974, the Flying Tiger Line officially dedicated its new world headquarters at Los Angeles International Airport during an open house. Wayne Hoffman, the Chairman of the Board, and his wife Laura, alongside Executive VP and Chief Operating Officer Joe Healy, together with veteran members including Captain Robert F. "Duke" Hedman, Joe Baker and Joe Cuppett, warmly welcomed the Tiger family. The star guest at the event was B.C. (Beautiful Cat), a two-year-old tigress. The original two-storey building (nicknamed Lo Tiger by Joe Baker) was situated beside the new ten-storey Hi Tiger building. The open house drew 1,500 Tigers and their families who explored every corner of Hi Tiger and the renovated Lo Tiger, as well as touring the hangar and flight training centre. Various employees played key roles as guides and hosts, contributing to the day's success. Visitors experienced a DC-8 simulator ride and they had a rare opportunity to see the 10th floor offices of corporate executives and financial staff. The maintenance hangar featured the DC-8-63CF N799FT, leased from Overseas National Airways from September 1973 to June 1974, and still adorned in a basic Air Siam livery.   J. Eyerman

Flying barnyards. In June 1974, two DC-8s were converted into flying barnyards to transport 212 Santa Gertrudis breeding cattle from Florida to the Philippines. The aircraft were fitted with an aluminum gating system and special floor coverings were topped with wood shavings. The cargo included young heifers weighing in at around 700lbs each, while the young bulls tipped the scales at 1,000lbs. The cattle, raised on the Big B Ranch in Belle Glade, Florida and the renowned King Ranch in Texas, were chosen to help the Philippines reach its goal of achieving one cow per Filipino, totalling 40 million cattle. The Philippine government was aiming for self-sufficiency in meat supplies by prioritising livestock production. Flying Tigers facilitated the transportation in two 24-hour-long flights from Miami to Mactan Airport in Cebu. The Santa Gertrudis were selected for their excellent beef production and ability to withstand hot climates. Developed by the King Ranch, this breed, a combination of Shorthorn (Lavender Viscount) with a bit of Brahman for durability, was recognised by the USDA in 1940 as the first pure American breed of beef cattle.

747 Freight Master. Accepting Flying Tiger Line's first Boeing 747 Freight Master in Wichita, Kansas on August 28, 1974, Tiger Board Chairman Wayne M. Hoffman and President Robert W. Prescott, right, receive the key to the aircraft from E. H. "Tex" Boullioun, president of Boeing Commercial Airplane Company. Boeing employees painted the tiger shark mouth on the nose to recall the colourful founding of the all-cargo airline by Prescott and eleven other veterans of the famed World War II Flying Tiger fighter unit. Upon arrival at Los Angeles in the early morning hours of August 29, the tiger shark artwork was removed. The crew on the flight from Wichita to Los Angeles were Captains Howell Rickman and Oakley Smith, senior director of flying, Second Officers M. J. Barnwell and Al Grant, manager second officers.

Part of the Tiger maintenance team which, over the course of five months, spent more time in Wichita than at home; from left to right: Bill Pieper, project engineer; Wayne Hoffman; Rhuel Trimble, Inspection; Dave McElroy, Flying Tigers resident service engineer, Robert W. Prescott; Vice President Maintenance John McDonald and Snr Director of Engineering Chuck Steeves.

Photos Laurie Fish

A team effort. Tigers met with Boeing officials in Wichita as modifications to the first Tiger 747 neared completion. Left, Beverly Lancaster, assistant general manager, Wichita; Tom Delaney, Tiger VP-Customer Services; Boeing VP and general manager-Wichita Otis Smith; Tiger VP-Maintenance John McDonald; Tiger VP-Operations Jim Colburn; Boeing rep Fred Carol and Bill Pieper, senior Tiger rep on the 747 project based in Wichita. The Tiger team condensed preparations for the new aircraft's maintenance, ground support, training and material control, completing the tasks in a quarter of the time taken by other airlines. Boeing President "Tex" Boullioun credited the success to great teamwork and acknowledged the crucial role of the Wichita group and constant support from Tiger personnel.

New Terminal, New 747 Service. On September 10, 1974, sunshine greeted the new Tiger terminal at John F. Kennedy International Airport. The day commemorated two significant milestones for Flying Tiger Line: the dedication of the JFK terminal and a reception for the inaugural flight of the Boeing 747, N800FT, to Chicago, Anchorage, Tokyo and Taipei. Approximately 2,000 guests toured the 10-acre terminal, which showcased its international and domestic capabilities, including the simultaneous handling of three DC-8-63Fs or two DC-8s and a 747. The facility, designed for Tiger operations, featured an all-electric interior materials handling system, a 320ft travelling elevator system, a contained bypass system for full containers, powered jacks and electric forklifts. This state-of-the-art terminal had consolidated New York operations, offering increased capacity, speed and efficiency in cargo handling. In the picture, fourth and fifth from the left are Laura Hoffman and her husband Flying Tigers Board Chairman Wayne Hoffman with Robert W. Prescott, President of the Flying Tiger Line. On the left of Prescott are Audrey Healy and her husband Executive Vice President-Chief Operating Officer Joseph J. Healy, and Richard L. "Dick" Haberly, General Manager JFK.

Inaugural 747 flight to Tokyo. After departing John F. Kennedy International Airport, the 747 stopped in Chicago and Anchorage before proceeding across the ocean to Tokyo, where traditional Daruma ceremonies marked the aircraft's arrival on September 11, 1974. The Daruma, a hollow round doll, brightly painted except for the eyes, symbolizes the ability to "bounce back" from hardship and are regarded as a talisman of good luck. At the beginning of a task one eye is painted and upon completion, the other eye is filled in, indicating success. In this case, one eye of a Daruma was painted at JFK when the inaugural flight began. Above, second from right, Russ Emerson, vice president-Asia, paints in the other eye, marking the 747's first successful trip to Japan. With Emerson are, from left, Paul Stokes, General Manager-Asia; Second Officer Al Grant; and Captains Oakley Smith and Howell Rickman.

Strange cargo. In September 1974, a particularly unusual shipment was dispatched to the Republic of China via a Flying Tiger Line DC-8-63F jet freighter from San Francisco International Airport. The cargo destined for Taipei, Taiwan, comprised 30 young fallow deer intended for breeding. Their horns were to be processed into valuable elixirs and aphrodisiacs. Acquired from the Holiday Island Exotic Animal Park near Eureka Springs, Arkansas, the 18 bucks and 12 does were bought by Hong Kong exporter Henry S. Woo of China Overseas for a private farm in Hsin Chu, Taiwan. The horns, which are shed in the spring, are sliced and ground to extract medicine, known as "loh yuh tsin", which was regarded as a potentially significant medical discovery, akin to acupuncture. Chinese herbalists combine this extract with hundreds of herbs, claiming it can help cure anaemia, tired blood, old age and even restore sexual vigour.

Persistent ghosts. When the first two 747-123Fs were delivered to Flying Tigers they still bore remnants of their former owner's identity. American Airlines' "ghost" letters persisted on the metal even after the paint had been stripped away. Eliminating them proved to be a challenging task for the maintenance team. In late 1974, various polishes were tested until one was found that was up to the job. The metal polish was meticulously applied and buffed, with each letter taking approximately 1½ hours to eradicate. Once complete, the Flying Tigers' lettering was accentuated with a 2¼-inch white border. M. McNelly

The second Flying Tiger's 747. Originally built in 1970 for American Airlines with the registration N9662, Flying Tiger's 747, N801FT, was approaching completion as a freighter at Boeing's Wichita plant in September 1974.

Men make it official. On October 22, 1974, 18 new Flying Tiger flight attendants were awarded their wings and diplomas at a graduation luncheon at the Nut Tree restaurant near Sacramento. The newly-trained FAs had just finished a rigorous, two-week training programme directed by instructor Marilyn Breen at the Tiger facility at nearby Travis Air Force Base. What set this class apart was the inclusion of three men, marking the first time male flight attendants had graduated from formal FT training in over 20 years. A brief discussion between Doug Smith, senior director of operations, and Marge Hough, chief flight attendant, clarified that while men had served as Tiger FAs on early passenger flights, these three were officially recognised as the first men to complete formal FT flight attendant training. In 1974, the Air Transport Association of America reported that, out of over 41,000 flight attendants flying for U.S. airlines, approximately 2,500 were men. From back, left to right: Betty Carver, Marilyn Breen, Lynn Everett, Debbie Weston, Lisa Peterson, Norma Sandoval, Linda Eaton, Candy Clair, Mary Sullivan, Beatriz Patino, Victoria Plimpton, Kenneth Barton, Marge Hough, Karen Holliman, Brenda Brown. Kneeling: Steve Street, seated, Kathy Jeffery, Sue Brady, Barbara Ganzkow, Guia Academia, kneeling, Deanne O'Halloran. In front, kneeling: Patricia Burke and Roger Peake.   Colleen Ferguson

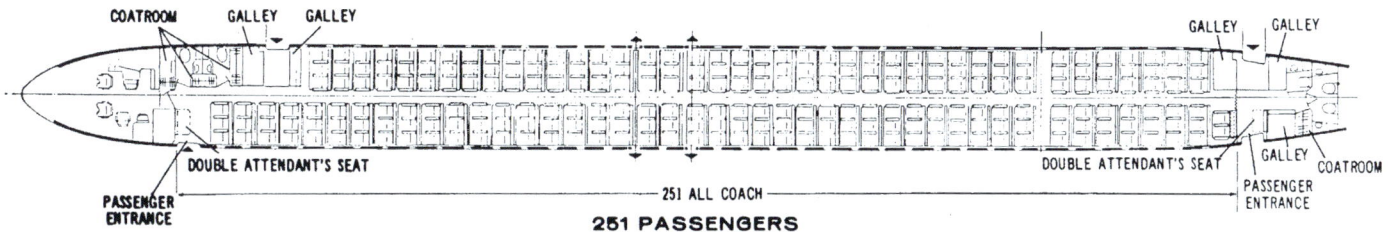

Wings over Yokota. Flying Tiger Line DC-8-63CF N798FT in October 1974 at Yokota Air Base, Japan, a major United States Air Force base west of Tokyo. Originally delivered to American Flyers Airline in 1970, N798FT was purchased a year later by Flying Tigers together with sistership N797FT. The aircraft could accommodate 251 passengers in an all-economy configuration, with six flight attendants.   Kenneth Barton

Ingenuity works wonders. Flying Tigers were dissatisfied with conventional methods of transporting Pratt & Whitney JT9D engines for the Boeing 747. Surface shipping was deemed too time consuming, and the "podding" technique, involving mounting the engine on another aircraft's wing, was both costly and labour intensive. The alternative, carrying the engine inside the 747 freighter itself, posed challenges due to weight, size and stability issues. Dick Feuerherm, freight handling instructor (pictured on the right in a blue shirt), devised a solution. With technical assistance from Ralph Foster, supervisor of facilities and equipment planning, they created an air shipping stand with removable wheels. This innovation allowed the engine to be moved on the ground and, without the wheels, loaded directly onto the aircraft's main cargo deck, where it was secured in one of four positions. The first 747 engine was loaded onto a Tiger aircraft, flown to JFK and, impressively, offloaded in just seven minutes.

Disney takes Tigers to Hong Kong. Unusual events unfolded in early 1975 when two chartered Tiger DC-8-63Fs transported costumes and sets for the popular "Disney on Parade" travelling show from Perth, Australia to Hong Kong. Upon unloading at Hong Kong's Kai Tak Airport, Alice-in-Wonderland, Pluto, Goofy and the inimitable Mickey Mouse surprised and entertained Tigers and airport personnel. After the performances in Hong Kong, the sets and costumes were once again loaded onto Tigers for a trip to Taipei. The nearly year-long tour of the show also included stops in Tokyo, Bangkok, Singapore, Jakarta and Manila before returning to Australia.

Hazardous Duty. On March 2, 1975, under a U.S. government contract, Flying Tigers initiated rice airlifts from Saigon to Phnom Penh, supporting war-stricken Cambodia where food supplies had been severed by advancing communist forces. For 43 days, volunteer crews and ground support personnel prioritised the Cambodians' plight, conducting between two and six aid flights a day. Despite challenging conditions, Tigers made 176 landings at Phnom Penh's Pochentong Airport, delivering a total of 16,687,265lbs of rice. Ground personnel in Saigon, led by Gary Kangieser, managed the operation very efficiently, handling significant cargo volumes. Unfortunately, the U.S. evacuation of Phnom Penh on April 12 marked the end of the ricelift, leaving Tiger crews saddened that they had been unable to continue their mission of mercy.

Archie Hall

In flak jackets and helmets, the front office comprised Captain Tage "Ted" Brondum, First Officer Kenny Johnson, Second Officer Archie Hall, Flight Mechanic Richard "Rich" Hernandez, with CBS News New York photographer Udo Nesch riding along on the jumpseat.

Captain William Bill Towner

Second Officer Archibald W. "Archie" Hall posing in front of DC-8-63AF N783FT sporting First Officer Larry Partridge's hand-applied lettering "Phnom Penh Ph Nancy", named after his wife. N783FT played a crucial role in the ricelift operation. Grant Schwartz and his team of Vietnamese team members worked tirelessly throughout the nights, replacing tyres and brakes, and repairing numerous bullet holes - 278 on a single flight.   Photos Archie Hall

First Officer Kenneth G. "Kenny" Johnson

Tigers Leave Vietnam. Amidst the deteriorating situation in South Vietnam, Flying Tigers executed a bold evacuation from Saigon on April 20, 1975. Piloted by Captain Ralph Mitchell (above left), First Officer Ted Freedel (above right), and Second Officer Rick Middel (middle right), Tiger DC-8-63CF N791FT flew to Tan Son Nhut Airport from Bangkok. The mission was to rescue key personnel, including Station Manager Gary Kangieser, Maintenance Representative Grant Swartz (below right with blue hat), 12 Vietnamese Tiger employees and 29 dependents. Notably, they also provided passage to a group of U.S. and Vietnamese citizens, including staff from World Airways, Trans International (TIA) and American Express. The decision to evacuate was prompted by U.S. officials warning that there could be enemy rocket attacks within 48 hours. The meticulous plan involved feigning mechanical issues, notifying Tigers and their families, and executing a covert night evacuation. Passengers clung to cargo nets during takeoff, bound for Guam. While the DC-8 resumed regular cargo service to Hong Kong, the group travelled to Hawaii for immigration clearance before landing in Los Angeles on April 26. The media were on hand to record their arrival - showcasing the resilience and resourcefulness of the Flying Tigers. Photos Captain Ralph Mitchell

Orient skies. Captain Mark Devereaux captured a dramatic shot in June 1975, depicting two Tiger DC-8 tails set against the distinctive Taipei, Taiwan skyline, encapsulating the Flying Tigers' passage through the Orient.

Special order. In June 1975, Flying Tigers transported two horses from Anchorage to Los Angeles on a regular scheduled DC-8-63 jet freighter flown by N793FT. This seemingly routine operation was noteworthy because the airline did not have authorisation from the Civil Aeronautics Board (CAB) to pick up or discharge cargo in Anchorage, despite most transpacific flights passing through there. To facilitate the service, Flying Tigers secured a special exemption from the CAB. The approval highlighted the absence of a scheduled freighter service between ANC and LAX and the inability of carriers in Anchorage to accommodate horses on their existing flights. Subsequently, Flying Tigers obtained CAB approval for scheduled freighter services, allowing them to take advantage of their newly acquired 32,000 square foot terminal in Anchorage. The horses, owned by Kathleen Nelson of Anchorage, were loaded into specialised stalls, accompanied by an attendant and flown to Los Angeles. From there, they were transloaded onto a smaller charter aircraft for the continuation of their journey to Guadalajara, Mexico. The photograph shows the horses being loaded in Anchorage, with from left to right: Billy Rowe, operations supervisor; Toni Trudeau, handler; Harold Haynes, station agent; Roy Lynn, station agent; and Tom Pagels, part-time station agent. Crew members Rory G. Pendley, First Officer on the left and John A. Binikos, Second Officer were observing the procedure.

Conquering new heights. On July 13, 1975, Flying Tigers' 747-123F N801FT took off from Tokyo, heading to Anchorage with 205,000lbs of freight, marking a record load on the TYO-ANC route since the introduction of the Freight Master. The remarkable payload was attributed, in part, to the installation of new shelf pallets. These innovative units were developed by Flying Tigers employees, among them Dick Feuerherm (pictured), to optimize the aircraft's 20,750 cubic foot main deck capacity and its ten-foot high side cargo door.

Tiger's frozen pause. This dramatic shot captured a Tiger DC-8-63CF, N792FT, parked at Anchorage, Alaska, during an operational stop. The snow-covered ramp, the ice fog in the background and the deserted scene set the stage for an outstanding photo.

Kenneth Barton

Critical noise. This photograph, taken in January 1975, shows Flying Tigers Boeing 747-123F N801FT featuring "blow-in" door cowls on its engines. In 1975, Flying Tigers replaced the cowls on all three of its 747 jet freighters (N800FT, 801 and 802) with quieter units. This upgrade was necessary to enhance operational flexibility, particularly for flights to and from airports with noise-related curfews, such as Hong Kong's Kai Tak, where this shot was taken. Replacing these cowls enabled Flying Tigers' 747s to fully comply with both FAR Part 36 and the international noise regulation Annex 16.

Evolution of Identity. In early 1976, a noticeable change began to appear across the airline's fleet of DC-8-63Fs in a move towards a standardised image. The Flying Tiger Line name, previously displayed on the side of the aircraft, was modified to simply read 'Flying Tigers', the update being systematically implemented on each DC-8 as it underwent regular maintenance at the Los Angeles headquarters. Various names, including The Flying Tiger Line, Inc., Flying Tiger Line, Flying Tigers, Flying Tiger, Tigers, Tiger, were present on equipment, containers, stationery supplies and other company-branded items but in 1975, 'Flying Tigers' emerged as the most frequently used and generally preferred name among employees. The corporate name, Flying Tiger Line, Inc., continued to be used for business or legal reasons, akin to the practices of TWA/Trans World Airlines and Pan Am/Pan American World Airways. Notably, all the 747s had already joined the fleet with the Flying Tigers' name. This shot was taken in Los Angeles in July 1977 and the former "Line" is still visible.

Jacques Guillem Collection

Deadheading. Flying Tiger Line Flight Attendants Cheryl Lee and Marty Chapin deadheading on a ferry flight aboard DC-8-63 N798FT in 1976.
Kenneth Barton

Sky skaters. In April 1977, Flying Tigers DC-8-63CF N797FT was chartered from Phoenix to Honolulu by the Ice Capades travelling show. Based around theatrical ice skating performances, the shows often featured former Olympic and US National Champion figure skaters who had retired from formal competition. Started in 1940, the Ice Capades were enormously popular drawing millions of fans each year but public enthusiasm began to wane in the 1980s and the company went out of business in around 1995. From left to right: chorus girls Elisabeth Sadleir and Karol Daron, figure skater Hans Müller with his skating partner Darlene Ripepe 'Pepe,' and Christie Adams, advance publicist.

Upon arrival in Honolulu, Ice Capades performers and personnel deplaned through the rear door while their show sets and equipment were being off-loaded through the cargo door at the front of DC-8-63CF N797FT. Combination passenger-cargo flights were a specialty of the Tigers' charter operations.

Photos Mun Wong

Heat, Humidity, and High Fashion. Flight Attendants Barbara Ganzkow, Guia Academia, Kenneth Barton and Terri Jacobsen engaged in a light-hearted moment at Kadena Air Base, on the island of Okinawa in June 1976. It wasn't all fun though, Kenneth recalled the challenges of long round-trips from Yokota Air Base, in western Tokyo. A typical duty day involved a flight to Marine Corps Air Station at Iwakuni, then to Kadena, and finally back to Iwakuni, before returning to Yokota; a trip that, with ground time, lasted about twelve hours. The work was particularly gruelling during Japan's summer heat and humidity. The lack of available portable air-conditioning units for DC-8s at U.S. bases in Japan caused cabin temperatures to soar above 100 degrees when all the passengers had boarded and the cabin doors were closed. Clad in seventies-style brown polyester uniforms, the flight attendants experienced discomfort on the ground and in the air, at least until the aircraft's cooling system brought down the cabin temperature – just in time to land and swelter once again. Not only were the uniforms impractical because the fabric did not breathe but they also posed a fire hazard. Kenneth Barton, concerned for the cabin crews' safety, demonstrated just how dangerous the outfits could be in a fiery aircraft evacuation by taking a match to his uniform jacket in front of Flight Attendant Manager Brenda Brown. The polyester fabric quickly melted into gooey plastic, and Kenneth asked "How am I expected to evacuate passengers if I'm on fire?" This dramatic display prompted Flying Tigers to introduce new, dark green, fire-resistant wool uniforms.   Kenneth Barton

Crew dilemma. Difficult discussions took place on this DC-8-63 at Shannon, Ireland in June 1976. The cabin crew had exhausted their duty time and were not legally permitted to operate the flight to Tehran, a charter for Bell Helicopter. During that era, crews had the option to negotiate with Crew Scheduling regarding extended duty. The six-strong crew was evenly split, with three in favour of exercising their contractual right to cancel and three wishing to continue to Iran. Ultimately, a unanimous decision was reached to proceed, thanks to an offer from Scheduling to deadhead them back home from Tehran via Pan Am. This arrangement included a three-day layover at the Excelsior Hotel in Rome. The Pan Am flight was a 707 route from Tehran to Damascus, Beirut (if conditions permitted landing), Rome, and finally, New York. Pictured from left: Erika Bessemer, Patty Burke, Steve Street and Senior Flight Attendant Lora Di Renzo.

Kenneth Barton

First retiring 747 captain. Stuart "Stu" J. McMahon, a veteran with 27 years' service, was the first Flying Tigers 747 captain to retire, at the mandatory age of 60 for pilots. His final flight, from Tokyo to Seattle on Flying Tigers' 747 N800FT was marked by informal farewell gatherings in Tokyo and Seattle. At least his last duty flight was an uneventful one, a fact he acknowledged to crew members Al Brown, first officer; and Vic Newman, second officer. Upon landing in Seattle, the tower, tipped off by the airline's HQ, congratulated him and offered to vector him anywhere he desired. Stu, reflecting on his diverse career flying 27 different aircraft, named the DC-8-63F as his favourite from the airline's fleet. Before joining Flying Tigers in 1949, Stu served as a civilian flight instructor for the U.S. Navy and became a test pilot for Douglas Aircraft in 1942. George Brownfield, Cascade Newsphoto Svs

Cathay Pacific Collaboration. In June 1976, Flying Tigers and Cathay Pacific Airways embarked on a joint venture by inaugurating an all-cargo service from the United States to Singapore and Malaysia. This significant development was facilitated by the deployment of Cathay's Boeing 707-351C jet freighters, which had recently been converted from passenger configuration. As the flag carrier of Hong Kong, Cathay Pacific strategically introduced the Boeing 707 jet freighter into service, establishing connections between the Crown Colony and destinations such as Seoul, Singapore, Bangkok and Kuala Lumpur. The collaboration operated four times a week, with Flying Tigers' 747s and DC-8s linking with Cathay Pacific's 707-351C freighter bound for Singapore, thereby offering U.S. exporters a same-day, all-cargo service. The cooperative effort extended further as Flying Tigers' aircraft met Cathay's freighter in Seoul three days a week. In addition to Singapore, the 707 cargo jet extended its route to Kuala Lumpur, providing another interline route for Flying Tigers. The picture shows a Cathay Pacific Cargo's 707-351C being towed to the ramp behind 747-123F N801FT, positioned in front of the Hong Kong Air Cargo Terminal. Ray Cranbourne

Elevated comfort. Horses are loaded into padded shipping stalls which are then lifted into the cargo compartment of the DC-8-63AF by a mobile unit.

Dynamic identity. The registration N111NA has been worn by four different TigerAir (formerly called National Aircraft Leasing) BAC 1-11 401AKs between 1973 and 1977: c/n 055, 065, 060 and 086 respectively. Originally N5040 with American Airlines, N111NA (c/n 086) was pictured at Brussels in June 1976, operating corporate flights with Tiger Leasing Group.   Guy Viselé

BAC ONE-ELEVEN

Flying Tigers flies a tiger. How appropriate that Flying Tigers was chosen to transport the celebrity tiger, Gombi, from Los Angeles to Manila in July 1976. Pictured with trainer-actress Susan Backlinie, Gombi was making the 22-hour trip to the Philippines to appear in Francis Ford Coppola's 'Apocalypse Now', the Vietnam War-era epic starring Marlon Brando, Robert Duvall and Martin Sheen. The handsome five-year-old tiger was owned by Monty Cox of Lion Wild Animal Rentals in Ventura, California. Cox and Miss Backlinie accompanied Gombi to Manila onboard DC-8-63AF N784FT for his two to three week acting assignment. As with most movie stars, Gombi was watching his diet to keep movieland trim, consuming a mere 15lbs of meat and chicken per day. The tiger was fed five raw chickens before his flight. Pack Air (international freight forwarders) handled arrangements for the shipment, coordinating with Flying Tigers' Los Angeles customer service representative Toni III, to keep tabs on the tiger throughout its 12:30 a.m. departure. Flying Tigers had earlier also transported camera equipment, explosives and a helicopter that would be used in Coppola's iconic movie. Bill Hilliard

Missing link? Once promoted as anthropology's missing link, Oliver the Humanzee was another unusual cargo delivered by Flying Tigers. In July 1976, he was on board flight 071, operated by N801FT, from New York Kennedy to Tokyo. Standing at four feet six inches and weighing 120lbs, Oliver, owned by New York attorney Michael Miller, displayed characteristics that intrigued scientists. Walking upright with a man-like posture, he also exhibited higher intelligence and had a distinct bone structure that set him apart from typical primates – his baldness further added to his mystique. Miller assembled a panel of experts to study Oliver's origins and characteristics. During his five-week stay in the Orient, Oliver participated in experiments, television shows and a documentary. Comfortably seated in the upper deck area of the 747-123F, JFK secretary Barbara Berkey (pictured) served a roast beef sandwich and orange juice to the star guest. After the cameras had left, Oliver was placed into a large cage for the flight from JFK to Tokyo. His trip abroad drew extensive media coverage, with over 40 newspapers in Japan featuring the chimp's photo and story.   Chuck Slade

New Tiger tails. Time for a change – in December 1976, it was decided that Flying Tigers' 747 and DC-8-63 jet freighters would receive a new tail design. Out went the longstanding Circle T symbol and in came contemporary FLYING TIGERS lettering in white on a blue background. The shift began in Asia, where the sales force was finding the circled letter T was less effective in communicating with potential customers. Recognising the limitations of putting a tiger's face on the tail, the airline opted for a cleaner design that provided immediate identification in various contexts. Coincidentally, Trans International Airlines also shifted from its TIA logo to display the parent company's bold T symbol on their DC-10 and DC-8 tails, emphasising a broader trend in airline branding. The first aircraft in the Tiger fleet to carry the new tail design was N797FT, spotted in Brussels before taking off from runway 01. Jacques Guillem Collection

Before and after. Flying Tigers' DC-8-63s, housed in the Los Angeles HQ maintenance hangar displayed the old and new. N797FT shows off the new tail design, while below, N788FT is still sporting the Circle T logo. The DC-8 tails were repainted as part of the routine maintenance schedule.

Orca across the pond. Heading for a bigger home, on October 28, 1976, a 19-foot, 5,500lb killer whale called Ramu was successfully transported from London's Windsor Safari Park to SeaWorld of San Diego, where he was renamed Winston. Having outgrown his London accommodation, it was hoped the nine-year-old Orca would contribute to breeding and research studies focusing on ageing, growth patterns and acoustical capabilities. A team of SeaWorld biologists, led by Dr. Lanny Cornell, and veterinarian Edward Asper, along with cetacean transportation expert Don Goldsberry, flew to London on October 27 to prepare for the transfer. The killer whale, which had been captured from the Puget Sound area of Seattle in 1970, was destined for SeaWorld's Shamu Stadium. Transported on Flying Tiger DC-8-63AF, N784FT, the 12-hour flight from London's Heathrow Airport was uneventful. The creature's wellbeing was ensured in a specially-designed transport unit, custom-made for the journey, keeping his skin moist, with vital signs being monitored by Dr. Cornell. No tranquilisers or drugs were used during the journey. The delicate offloading process in San Diego was observed by crew member Daniel "Danny" Anthony Dileo (on the right at door 1L).

Rodeo Show Charter. On February 13, 1977, Flying Tigers conducted a charter transporting livestock and personnel from The American Rodeo Show from Los Angeles to Taipei for performances in Taiwan. The aircraft, a DC-8-63CF registered N797FT, accommodated 29 horses, 8 bulls, 10 steers, 6 calves, 2 buffalo, and 12 American cowboys, as depicted in the photograph. Established in 1977 by Robert Floyd "Bob" Cook, the American Rodeo Show staged approximately 5,000 performances across four continents during the subsequent decade.

Military charter. In March 1977, Flying Tigers DC-8-63AF N790FT operated a military charter flight for the French army. The aircraft is illustrated above during a layover at Djibouti–Ambouli International Airport, just a few months before the country of Djibouti achieved independence from France on June 27. Jacques Guillem

From Delta to Tiger. Having taken delivery of the first three ex-American Airlines 747-123F aircraft, N800FT, #801 and #802, in 1974 and 1975, the next three "new" Tiger jumbo 747 freighters were former Delta Air Lines 747-132 passenger planes. An aircraft, believed to be N803FT, is pictured at Boeing's Wichita plant, nearing completion as a freighter while still adorned with a basic Delta Air Lines livery. N803FT was originally constructed in 1970 for Delta as N9897.

SeaWorld's Flying Ark. In May 1977, Shamu, a three-ton performing killer whale embarked on a cross-country journey aboard Flying Tigers DC-8-63CF N792FT, cleverly named the "SeaWorld Flying Tiger Orc-Ark". The flight covered 3,000 miles from San Diego, California, to another SeaWorld park in Aurora, Ohio. Accompanying Shamu was a diverse group of marine animals and birds, including nine dolphins, one elephant seal, 18 sea lions, three harbor seals, two otters, three macaws and an assortment of fish. Ron Rogers, positioned on the left of the tank and Glenn Van Winkle, crouched on the right side, served as the Flying Tigers' loadmasters and charter representatives for the operation. At the lower part of the picture, a SeaWorld staff member with a spray pump kept the animals moist before being loaded onto the aircraft.

Glenn Van Winkle

Cole of California. The Flying Tiger Line began transporting garments and women's clothing for Sears in 1946, and initially Douglas C-47s were fitted out with hangers so that full loads of clothing could be carried easily and efficiently. By 1977, the airline's marketing department had signed a contract with Cole of California, a renowned swimwear brand known for its stylish and innovative designs – seen being modelled in our photograph. The models are posed beside a garments-on-hangers container on the Los Angeles ramp in May 1977. This style of container proved to be a very time-saving and cost-effective solution for shippers.

Bill Varie

New 747 design unveiled. The first Boeing 747 to wear the new Flying Tigers tail design was photographed during a test flight above Seattle in June 1977 following the completion of its conversion from passenger to all-cargo configuration. Originally operated by Delta Air Lines as N9897 in October 1970, N803FT was delivered to Flying Tigers in July 1977. The airline's first three 747s, N800FT, #801 and #802, received the new markings while undergoing regular maintenance. Flying Tigers' new 747 titles included the Tiger face logo and slogan "The Airfreight Airline" near the aircraft's nose. The new addition replaced the original Freight Master, which the airline no longer used as a designation for the 747 freighters.

A captain's lens. Flying Tigers captain and amateur photographer Robert H. "Bob" Martin took this spectacular shot of a Tiger 747-100F on approach to Hong Kong's Kai Tak International Airport. The dramatic overland approach to Hong Kong was the only one of its kind in the world, and when weather conditions were good, it provided a memorable view of aircraft landing against the spectacular Hong Kong skyline. Captain Martin had been preparing to capture the image for quite some time. He first explored the airport area to find the right vantage point and then waited until one of his layovers coincided with good weather and an aircraft landing over the city. A former U.S. Navy aviator, Bob joined Flying Tigers in December 1946.

Crew corner

Journey back in time to March 1977 at Hong Kong Kai Tak International Airport, where Captain Charles E. "Chuck" Griffith, Second Officer Jean-Claude Démirdjian, and First Officer John W. Stebel embraced a uniquely unconventional uniform – walk shorts paired with long socks. Moments taken before their next flight, as they strolled the vibrant streets of Hong Kong, encapsulating an era of aviation charm and camaraderie.

On December 17, 1976, Senior Captain Robert F. "Duke" Hedman, holding the top position on the company's pilot roster, commanded a 747 for his final flight from Tokyo to Seattle. Duke, who initially joined Claire Lee Chennault's American Volunteer Group in China, became the first American "ace" of World War II by downing five enemy aircraft over Rangoon on Christmas Day, 1941. Duke piloted every type of aircraft operated by Flying Tigers, starting with the Budd Conestoga on August 21, 1945.

In June 1977, Captain Gerry Proctor and First Officer Tom Constable, strapped into their DC-8-63F on the ground in Dubai after a cattle charter, prepared to push back in scorching temperatures of 104 degrees Fahrenheit (40 degrees Celsius). The intense heat prompted them to remove their shirts.

Crowds of friends and associates gathered in New York, Detroit and Los Angeles in June 1977 as Captain James "Jim" A. Sanders flew from one farewell party to another during his last flight for the airline. In Los Angeles, as depicted above, Sanders disembarks from DC-8-63CF #781, on which maintenance friends had stenciled his name for the flight – a nice touch.

Cattle charter. The photograph, taken in June 1977, shows cattle from the Northern Territory being prepared for loading onto the DC-8-63CF N795FT at Darwin Airport, Australia, before a charter flight to Brunei. Tom Constable

Airfreight deregulation. United States President Jimmy Carter signed a bill on November 9, 1977 that essentially eliminated government regulation of domestic all-cargo air services. The bill, H.R. 6010 Air Cargo Deregulation, outlined requirements for entrance into the air freight business and removed Civil Aeronautics Board control over rates and routes. As a result, Flying Tigers agreed to purchase two additional DC-8-61 series jets for $12 million. Acquired from Overseas National Airways, DC-8-61CF N867FT (pictured at Pinal Air Park) and N868F (seen at Miami) joined the fleet in December 1977 to serve new U.S. domestic markets added as a result of airfreight deregulation legislation.   Photos Frank de Koster

Domestic expansion. After being confined for more than 20 years to a domestic route that limited Flying Tigers to the Northeast, the Midwest and the West, deregulation opened the door for service expansion to the Southeast and Southwest. To achieve this, the airline expanded its fleet with five more DC-8s, bringing the total to 20. It leased five additional DC-8-61CFs from Trans International Airlines between February 1978 and April 1979; N860FT, #861, #862, #863 and #864. N861FT, pictured at the top, flew for Tiger from June 1978 until May 1984 and operated with a white top. In return, Flying Tigers leased two DC-8-63CFs, N793FT and N794FT to TIA, resulting in a net increase of five aircraft. N793FT, pictured above, was leased to TIA from June 1978 to the end of September 1978, maintaining a Tiger fuselage with Trans International Cargo titles. The picture was taken in Zurich in September 1978.

Photos Jacques Guillem Collection

New tigresses. Karen I. Dillon (on the right) and Sandra D. Donnelly, inspecting a DC-8 main landing gear, were the second and third female pilots hired by the Flying Tigers, respectively on January 3 and January 23, 1978. Sandra later became the first (and only) female captain at Tigers on October 5, 1988, before the company was acquired by Federal Express. They were photographed in Los Angeles during a walk-around of DC-8-63AF N790FT.

Brett Fish

Robert W. Prescott, May 5, 1913 - March 3, 1978. Robert William Prescott, a visionary and stalwart pioneer of the air cargo industry, and a colourful World War II fighter ace, passed away on March 3, 1978, at his home after a two-year battle with cancer. The afternoon service, held on March 7 at the Encino Community Church in Southern California, were attended by more than 700 people. Following Bob's death, Wayne Hoffman became president of the Flying Tiger Line.

Key connections. On March 6, 1978, DC-8-61CF N862FT initiated twice-daily airfreight flights connecting Atlanta, Georgia and Charlotte, North Carolina, with departures to key destinations in the United States and Asia. The prime-time service left Atlanta's Hartsfield International Airport at 11:40 p.m. Monday through Friday, arrived in Charlotte at 12:30 a.m. Tuesday through Saturday, and then continued to Chicago, reaching O'Hare at 2:40 a.m. Seen in Atlanta, for the inaugural flight, from the left: unknown; Flying Tigers' Dave Edell, regional sales manager; Gayle Baxter, 1978 Dogwood Festival Queen; James "Jay" J. Tufts, Southern regional vice president; Pete Blewett, manager-terminal operations; and unknown. Gayle presented a dogwood tree, a symbol of Atlanta's welcome.

Texan tie-up. Flying Tigers began services to Houston and Dallas-Fort Worth with DC-8-61CF N862FT on April 3, 1978, linking two the state's biggest markets with others in the U.S. and Asia. Five weekly flights were operated to serve the two Texas markets. Flt. #441 took off from JFK at 9:30 p.m., flew to Chicago via Syracuse and Detroit, and then continued to Dallas and Houston in the early morning. Departing Dallas at 10 p.m., Flt. #440 arrived in Houston at 10:50 p.m., departed at 11:50 p.m., and terminated in Chicago at 2 a.m. Flt. #442 left Houston at 9:30 a.m., arrived in Chicago at 11:40 a.m. Chicago served as the domestic hub, connecting Flying Tigers flights to various destinations in its system. Special guests at Dallas/Fort Worth ceremonies included members of Robert Prescott's family, Mrs. Pauline Prescott, wife of Mr. Prescott's brother; and Mrs. Marguerite Lyon, Mr. Prescott's sister. Pictured Miss Transportation International Patty Carnes of Fort Worth drew the undivided attention of Flying Tigers inaugural flight crew members, from left to right, Gregory T. "Greg" Cotton, Second Officer; Robert L. "Bob" Baird, Captain and Franklin D. "Frank" Campbell, First Officer.

Flying start for Affirmed. Heading for the starting gate and victory at the 1978 Kentucky Derby, Affirmed, a three-year-old thoroughbred racehorse left Los Angeles on April 23, 1978, aboard a chartered Flying Tigers DC-8-63CF, bound for the Churchill Downs course in Louisville. The chestnut colt had participated in only four races leading up to the Kentucky Derby on May 6, winning first place in each Affirmed was owned by Mr. and Mrs. L. Wolfson of Harbor View Farms in Ocala, Florida. PATH Horse Transportation, Inc., based in Los Angeles, served as the official handling agent.

Barry Wrube

Meeting demand. Flying Tigers signed a one-year lease with World Airways to operate a 747-124F on July 1, 1978. The domestic deregulation of the airfreight industry had created demand for additional capacity. Previously, the 747 service had been limited to international routes. The new aircraft, N809FT, was inaugurated on July 17, providing nonstop wide-body scheduled service between San Francisco and New York (benefiting from the connectivity of the Tokyo flight in San Francisco, Monday through Friday) and also serving the Chicago market. From the East Coast, Flying Tigers offered shippers a flight departing from New York to San Francisco via Chicago. N809FT had originally been delivered to Continental Air Lines in May 1970 before being repurchased by Boeing and converted to a freighter in October 1975. The aircraft was then transferred to the Imperial Iranian Air Force (IIAF), later returned to Boeing in January 1978 and subsequently sold to World Airways in February 1978. N809FT retained its previous operator's (IIAF) green cheatline with the Tiger face logo and slogan "The Airfreight Airline" placed near the aircraft's nose.

CL44.com Archives

A close shave. On July 17, 1978, at 0330z, Flying Tigers DC-8-63CF N871TV, commanded by Captain Fred Lynch, with First Officer Tom Phiel and Second Officer Richard Dwyer, taxied for takeoff from Yokota Air Force Base, Japan, bound for Anchorage, Alaska. After blocking out, the aircraft initially taxied to the runway but was directed back to the ramp to remove a passenger in "customs hold". During this time, a mechanic noticed a low tyre and promptly replaced it while passengers and crew endured the hot weather on board. Unbeknownst to anyone, the adjacent tyre also required replacement. (Following the incident, stem valve tire pressure gauges were installed throughout the fleet.) At 0415z, with Captain Lynch at the controls, the aircraft taxied for departure. Approaching 100 knots, the tyres blew, causing the aircraft to shudder, and prompting Lynch to reject the takeoff. Photographs captured the blown tyres, magnesium wheel rims and brakes ablaze under the left wing. Despite the unexpected turn of events, all 219 passengers emerged unharmed, a testament to the professionalism of Senior Flight Attendant Marilyn Breen and the entire cabin crew, including Reita Tackitt, Teri Jacobson, Diane Woods, Leo One, and J. (Fay) Ewing. During the evacuation First Officer Tom Phiel attempted to address the folded escape slide at door L1 and amid the evacuation challenges, Captain Lynch, noticing Tom's missing tie, shouted a jibe from the bottom of the slide. Back at the company operations building, the crew members marked their survival with celebratory drinks sourced from the flight attendants' suitcases. Richard Dwyer

Pioneering Women. While in 1949 famed aviatrix Dianna Bixby had the distinction of being the first female to fly for the Flying Tiger Line, alongside Captain Dick Stratford, on a leased C-47 that she owned, Norah E. O'Neill earned her place in history as the first female hired by the Flying Tiger Line on December 1, 1976. She also became the world's first woman to operate the Douglas DC-8-63, serving as a flight engineer in 1977. Norah progressed to the position of first officer in September 1978, becoming the nation's pioneer woman to pilot heavy four-engine aircraft for a scheduled airline. Norah is seen in the cockpit of DC-8-63AF N786FT. Brownfield

High cube efficiency. Flying Tigers introduced a groundbreaking high cube container in October 1978 in a bid to optimize the interior space of its Boeing 747 freighters. The carrier's new container, AQ7, had a capacity of 773 cubic feet, a tare weight of 705lbs, and the ability to carry loads up to 15,000lbs. Other major carriers followed Flying Tigers' lead in acquiring this innovative container for more efficient cargo carriage. Dirk Feuerherm, Tiger's senior planner for cargo handling equipment, played a vital role in developing the sturdy, lightweight unit. The container's unique design enabled twenty high cube units to fit snugly in pairs down the centre of the main deck cargo compartment. With dimensions of 96 inches wide, 125 inches long and 118 inches high, the containers offered nearly four times the space of a standard LD3. Flying Tigers used them to transport various commodities from major Asian cities to the United States.

Brett Fish

Near miss in Chicago. Limited visibility greeted Captain Richard Petrick as he received clearance to land his 747 N804FT on runway 9R at Chicago's O'Hare International Airport on February 15, 1979. Traveling at around 115 miles per hour along the runway, a Delta Air Lines 727, N467DA, crossed the 747's path directly ahead. With remarkable instinct, Captain Petrick skillfully manoeuvered to the right, narrowly avoiding a collision. The 747 veered off the runway and crashed through a snow bank. The nose landing gear and engine #3 were torn off as the aircraft slid to a halt. Captain Petrick, including First Officer Dave Hooker and Second Officer Don Singer, and three deadheading passengers, successfully evacuated the aircraft without injuries. Miraculously, 115 individuals out on runway 9R were unharmed, thanks to Captain Petrick's quick reaction. The Delta plane continued its scheduled departure to Orlando, Florida. Investigations by the National Safety Transportation Board revealed that the O'Hare outbound ground controller's issuance of a taxi clearance across runway 9R permitted Delta 727-200 to move into a collision path with Tiger 747 and, further, that the Delta pilots failed to maintain a continuous vigil for landing traffic before entering an active runway. The improper clearance was the result of the ground controller's failure to see the displayed radar target of the landing aircraft.

Equipment gap. Flying Tigers 747-124F N809FT at Forbes Field in Topeka, Kansas in March 1979 on a refueling stop during a charter flight from El Paso, Texas to Shannon, Ireland. The airport had no trouble fueling the big aircraft but one piece of ground support equipment didn't quite fit the bill. The steps intended to access the main deck door fell around three to four feet short of providing full service. Rather than bridge the equipment gap, crew members chose to leave and enter via a built-in ladder aft of the nose gear. N809FT, originally delivered to Continental Air Lines in 1970, was wearing its former operator cheatline, the Imperial Iranian Air Force. Topeka Daily Capital staff, photo by Phil Schermeister

Making a point of flying together. Captain George Rayner, on the left; First Officer Frank Campbell, in the centre; and Second Officer Fred McClurkin completed a transcontinental flight on Flying Tigers DC-8-63AF N783FT in September 1979. At that time, Flying Tigers boasted ten black pilots, reportedly the highest percentage in the airline industry. Out of over 40,000 airline pilots in the USA, only 143 were black. The crew had bid for the flight with the aim of showcasing career opportunities available to black youth.

New Boeing. In August 1978, Wayne M. Hoffman, chairman of the board of Tiger International and Flying Tigers, announced the acquisition of two new Boeing 747-200Fs at a cost of about $115 million, including spare parts. The first aircraft, N806FT, was delivered on October 31, 1979. Flying Tigers had chosen Pratt & Whitney's JT9D-7Q engine and anticipated between 10 and 20 percent greater freight-carrying efficiency over the 747-100s then in operation, measured on a ton-mile basis. The airline had also taken options on four more aircraft, all to be powered by the JT9D-7Q . The new jetfreighter joined the airline's existing fleet of seven 747-100s and 21 stretched DC-8s. The 747-200F had the capacity to transport more than 240,000lbs of cargo at 575 miles per hour over a 3,600-mile range.

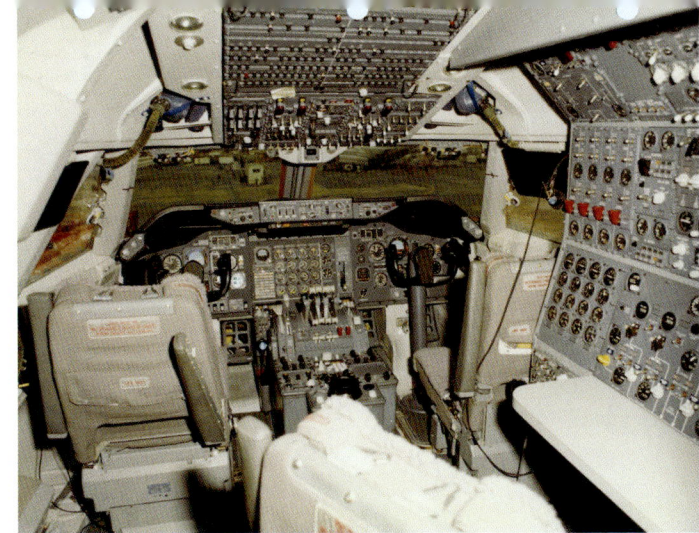

Inside the new 747-249F. These images were taken aboard N806FT "Robert W. Prescott" at Boeing's Everett Site in October 1979, before its delivery to Flying Tigers. The pictures on the left depict the newly outfitted cockpit and the flight engineer's panel. The cockpit was designed to accommodate two supernumeraries in addition to the regular crew. The pictures on the right show the upper deck configured to hold 19 passengers. Although twenty passenger seats had been installed, capacity was capped at 19, as exceeding this number would necessitate the presence of a flight attendant. Typically, the passengers consisted of employees, extra crew members, loadmasters, mechanics or veterinarians on animal charters.

Flying Tigers' pilot training. In 1979, training instructors in the back row, from left to right, were John Adcock, Jerry Petros, Ed Hatmaker, Ronald Cuiccio, Forrest King, and Bill Morrell. In the front row were Vince Torfin, supervisor of ground instruction and Earl Berbrick, manager of ground training. In the background were static displays of 747 aircraft instrumentation and systems to aid in crew member training.

Relief flight to Cambodia. Operating a mercy mission on November 24, 1979, Flying Tigers became the first U.S. commercial carrier to return to Phnom Penh ten months after the overthrow of the Pol Pot regime. Flying a chartered DC-8-63AF, the airline transported 77,000lbs of food, medicine and supplies sponsored by Operation California and the American Friends Service Committee. The relief flight resulted from intricate negotiations and planning to deliver aid directly from the U.S. despite the absence of formal recognition betwezen the two governments. Departing from Los Angeles on Thanksgiving Day, the trip to Phnom Penh took 31 hours, including stops in Anchorage, Japan and Hong Kong. Operation California organisers, Llewellyn Werner and Los Angeles attorney Richard Walden, spearheaded the effort. They secured clearance through the Cambodian Embassy in Moscow, UN diplomats and Cambodian officials. The flight, partially underwritten by actress Julie Andrews and her husband, producer Blake Edwards, carried over $1.5 million in supplies donated by Southern California companies. Despite challenges, the Flying Tigers crew, along with relief organisers and journalists, received a warm reception in Cambodia, fostering hopes for other aid missions. Pictured is Operation California organiser Llew Werner, left, being interviewed on the ramp at Flying Tigers' LAX terminal by Channel 7 newsman Fred Anderson.

Dedicated to Bob. Anne-Marie Prescott splashes champagne on the new 747-249F N806FT named after her husband "Robert W. Prescott". Joining her were, from the left: Vice President Public Relations Nissen Davis; Prescott's daughter Kirsten Smith; Flying Tigers' President Thomas "Tom" F. Grojean and his wife Terri; and Chairman Wayne Hoffman and his wife Laura. The ceremony, which took place in front of the headquarters maintenance hangar in Los Angeles on November 2, 1979, was witnessed by hundreds of Flying Tigers employees.

Paul Nowaske, Jon Proctor Collection

Tiger Country. In the seventies, Hong Kong was at the crossroads of Asia where anything you wanted or thought you ever wanted could be bought, sold or manufactured. It had been "Tiger Country" since 1968 when the airline opened an airfreight office in the old terminal building of Kai Tak International Airport. In this photo, taken from the roof of the Hong Kong Air Cargo Terminals Limited (HACTL) terminal, the brand new 747-249F N806FT "Robert W. Prescott" arrived in November 1979 on its maiden flight.

Earl Erickson

More Relief for Cambodia. On December 24, 1979, Flying Tigers DC-8-63AF, N790FT, departed Los Angeles International Airport with relief goods destined for Phnom Penh, Cambodia, marking the second such mercy flight in just over a month. Both flights had been organised by Operation California, a private initiative founded by two Los Angeles individuals, aiming to provide direct U.S. aid to Cambodia's starving population. The flights, labelled "Because We Care", carried 80,000lbs of emergency relief supplies, valued at over $1.5 million, including such essentials as baby formula and medical provisions. The departure was attended by California Governor Jerry Brown and a group of Southeast Asians, including a Buddhist priest who led a short prayer session. Fuel for the flight was partially donated by Shell Oil, and Flying Tigers facilitated a reduced rate, with the entire cost covered by private donations. Operation California's organisers, Llew Werner and Richard Walden, accompanied the freight to Cambodia, and they continued to work towards fundraising for more direct relief flights, including a celebrity benefit concert held in Los Angeles. Above, left to right, Second Officer Robert O. Duncan, Captain John Hess and First Officer Joel T. Osborne took the flight out of Los Angeles.

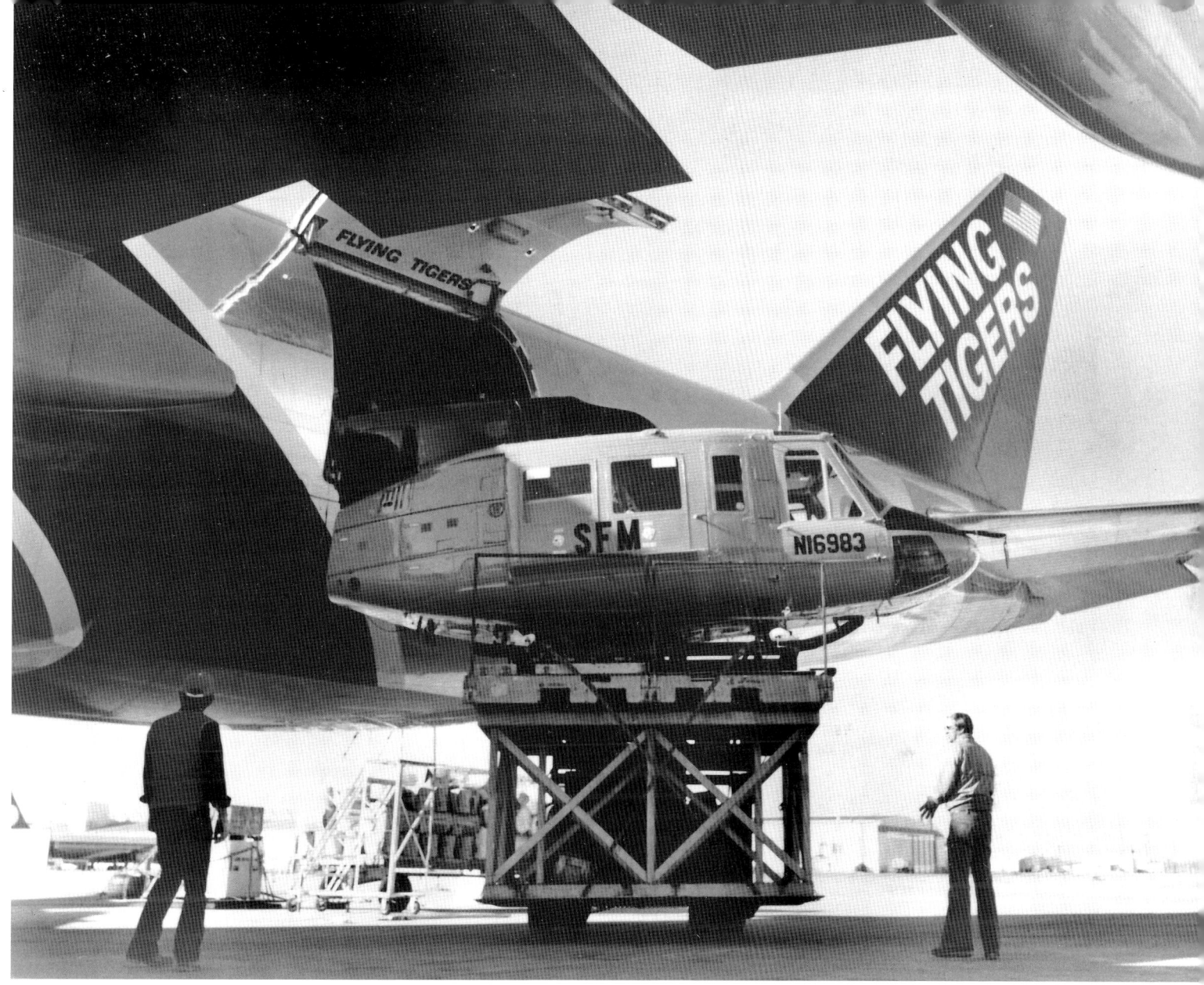

Peacekeeping Mission. American civilians, having maintained a peacekeeping vigil in the Sinai Desert for nearly four years, were able to expand their role in January 1980 with assistance from the Flying Tigers. The company transported three Bell 212 helicopters and short takeoff and landing (STOL) aircraft to the Sinai for E-Systems of Dallas, Texas. The aircraft were used by U.S. teams inspecting Egyptian military installations to ensure treaty compliance. The volunteers belonged to the Sinai Field Mission (SFM), which had monitored the Gidi and Mitla passes since February 22, 1976, under the Sinai II Agreement. The Egyptian-Israeli Peace Treaty, signed on March 26, 1979, dictated the termination of operations on January 25, 1980, following Israel's return of a portion of the peninsula captured during the 1967 war. E-Systems received a $13.3 million contract for continued involvement. A chartered Flying Tigers 747 jet freighter transported the cargo, including aircraft, construction materials and spare parts to Tel Aviv International Airport on January 18. In accordance with the treaty, U.S. teams inspected Egyptian military installations in the designated zone.

First 747 passenger flights. Flying Tigers was awarded a $25 million contract by the Intergovernmental Committee for European Migration (ICEM) in January 1980 to transport 7,000 refugees a month from Southeast Asia to the United States. Utilising a passenger 747-200B acquired from Singapore Airlines by sister company TigerAir Inc., the airline conducted approximately 13 flights a month over six months from April 1980. Passengers were collected from Bangkok, Singapore, Kuala Lumpur and Manila, ultimately arriving at Travis Air Force Base near San Francisco. The Singapore 747-212B, N747TA, had earlier been operated by Flying Tigers in December 1979 for a series of MAC charters, shuttling military personnel between San Diego, California and Okinawa, Japan. Preceding these flights, the Flying Tigers' maintenance department reconfigured the aircraft's interior to increase seating capacity from 390 to 458. These endeavours marked the inaugural 747 passenger flights in Flying Tigers' history. For the refugee charters, the airline's maintenance and engineering department again modified the interior, this time to accommodate 514 seats. The image above shows Flying Tigers flight attendants posing with Los Angeles ramp and maintenance personnel in front of N747TA before embarking on the first MAC trip. Subsequently, the Flying Tigers title was affixed to the aircraft's fuselage.

New Horizons Stateside. A new life awaited 550 Vietnamese and Laotian refugees in the United States as they disembarked from flight 7627 at Oakland. Expressionless, they patiently deplaned the 747-212B adorned in Navy blue, with both Flying Tigers and ICEM logos. Each family group carried a plastic bag containing all the necessary documents for entry into the United States: photos, passports, medical records, x-rays and birth certificates. Their journey took them from Bangkok to Hong Kong, Anchorage and finally Oakland, where they were bussed to the (inactive) Hamilton Air Force Base to complete the final paperwork. Refugees stayed at Hamilton until scheduled on a commercial flight to their ultimate destination, usually within a day or two.   Roger Foley

The Tiger Spirit. A comic strip spotlighting the company's main goals and programmes made its debut in the monthly Tigereview publication in March 1980. It showcased the new "Tiger Spirit", which was intended to embody the "can-do" attitude that had sustained the airline through some improbable challenges since 1945, solidifying its status as the world's premier airfreight carrier. The new-look tiger symbol featured in the Tiger Tales cartoon series and on items such as patches, T-shirts, lapel pins, bumper stickers and decals. Throughout the Flying Tigers offices, the image became a cherished identifier, adorning photos, porcelain, posters and even cuddly toys. The cartoon tiger, characterised by resourcefulness, friendliness and dedication, aimed to encapsulate the collective ethos of the workforce. The introduction of the new Tiger Spirit did not supplant the Tiger Face logo as the official service mark of the airline.

Terminal snapshot. A close-up of the brand-new Boeing 747-249F N806FT "Robert W. Prescott" on the Flying Tigers terminal ramp in Los Angeles in May 1980.

Brett Fish

Tigers' new 747. Flying Tigers took delivery of N808FT, named "William E. Bartling", on July 3, 1980, when it landed at Los Angeles International Airport. The new aircraft, named in honour of one of the airline's founders, became the third 747-249F in Flying Tigers' fleet – it already operated two 747-200Fs, six 747-100Fs and 21 stretched DC-8s at that time. The image shows the gleaming N808FT during the early hours of July 1980.

Shark mouth P-40 tribute. Tiger International Inc. acquired a vintage World War II P-40E Warhawk in July 1980. Originally registered as N41JR, it was disassembled, restored and reassembled by the TigerAir's Service Center at the Burbank Airport. Re-registered N41JA in September 1980, it was named after Robert W. Prescott to pay homage to the Flying Tiger Line founder. In December 1983, it was re-registered as N40FT, and from 1987 to 2011 the aircraft was loaned to the San Diego Air and Space Museum. Following acquisition by Tiger International Inc., the plane was transferred to the Federal Express Corporation in October 1989, maintaining its N40FT registration. In 2010, it found a new home at the Pacific Aviation Museum on Ford Island, Honolulu, where it remains on display. P-40E N41JR was photographed at its new home base with TigerAir in Burbank in July 1980.   James Collison

We've Got the World Together. Flying Tigers and Seaboard World Airlines took their first coordinated steps towards a merger agreement on July 18, 1979. Having gained support from key government departments it became official on October 1, 1980, and encountered no opposition from other airlines on anti-competitive grounds. Flying Tigers had been planning to independently expand into Europe, but considered the coalition, with each company excelling in different regions, would be more efficient and economical. The newly merged Flying Tigers fleet featured twenty-one DC-8s and sixteen 747s, serving over 30 airports worldwide. At the time, Seaboard's DC-8-63CFs were already leased to other airlines. Notably, before the repaint and re-registration process, Flying Tigers titles were applied to the four Seaboard 747-245Fs "Containerships", registered as N701SW, #702, #703 and #704. These were subsequently repainted in full Flying Tigers livery and re-registered as N811FT, #812, #813 and #814, respectively. A retitled Seaboard World 747-245F (N704SW) is pictured at Paris Charles de Gaulle. Christian Volpati

Dedicating the Henry L. Heguy. Employees gathered at New York Kennedy Airport's cargo terminal building 260 on October 17, 1980, to see Flying Tigers 747-245F, N816FT, being dedicated to "Henry L. Heguy". In keeping with the airline's tradition of naming its new 747s in honour of founders and pioneers, the freighter paid tribute to one of the pioneers of Seaboard & Western Airlines, later known as Seaboard World Airlines. As well as N815FT, named "W. Henry Renninger", the aircraft was on order for Seaboard at the time of the merger. Jane Heguy, Henry Heguy's widow, christened the new aircraft with champagne – she is photographed climbing the ladder with Executive Committee Chairman Richard Jackson who conducted the ceremony. Henry L. Heguy, navigator on Seaboard's inaugural commercial flight in 1947, played a crucial role in the airline's development until his death in 1975.

Charter to Oman. Flying Tigers handled a 747 charter from Basel to Muscat, Oman in 1980. The load comprised approximately 100 tons of pharmaceuticals and a Heliswiss Bell 206B JetRanger II helicopter, as seen above being loaded through the nose of Flying Tigers' 747-249F N810FT, which was named "Clifford G. Groh" after former AVG pilot and one of the airline's founders. Claude A. Iselin

Pipeline to Mexico. Around 202,650lbs of flexible rubber pipe filled the massive main deck of 747-249F N806FT "Robert W. Prescott" on a November 1980 charter flight #8000 from London to Mexico City. The pipe, shown above during the delicate off-loading process, was destined for duty in Mexico's growing oil drilling industry. The oddly shaped freight travelled from London to New York JFK and then JFK to Mexico City. Charter operations supervisors overseeing the process were Dick Dunn and Chuck Collins, assisted by Maintenance Representative Lenny Sulewski. At the controls of the 747, from London to JFK, were Captain Daniel Cork, First Officer Scott Cutler and Second Officer Robert Bologna; and from JFK to Mexico City, Captain Byron O'Hara, First Officer Leslie Johnson and Second Officer Thomas Schultz.

Crew corner

DC-8-63CF N793FT flight #144 bound for Boston via New York left Los Angeles International Airport on February 29, 1980 with 105,364lbs on board including six horses en route to New York from New Zealand. At the controls were, left to right, Captain Scott Simpson, Second Officer Dan Carpenter and First Officer Mike Coppola.

Out on the charter circuit (from left), Captain Henry P. "Hank" Germain, a 1957 Tiger veteran, First Officer Derek Younkin and Second Officer Tim Mooney brought flight #5059 from Frankfurt, Germany to Zurich, Switzerland on March 9, 1980 and on to New York Kennedy via Shannon, Ireland and Gander, Newfoundland.

Captain Ron Hall, Second Officer John Dill and First Officer Ron Voges get ready for take-off onboard a 747-212B passenger flight in December 1980.

During the early 1980s, Captains Howard L. "Howie" Harder and Calvin L. "Cal" Holderman, with Second Officer Robert X. "Bob" Lane explored Europe, the Middle East and Asia under a "Charter Domicile" agreement on DC-8s. The crew wore keffiyehs purchased in Riyadh as they performed their duties. Bob recalled, "We garnered stares while transiting the KLM crew centre and immigration in Amsterdam." Bob Lane

Metro International Takes Off. Metro International Airways, Flying Tigers' passenger division, was created in December 1980 and began charter services with the three former Singapore Airlines 747-212Bs and one stretched DC-8. Flying Tigers pilots, flight attendants and maintenance personnel operated and maintained Metro International's aircraft. Flights from New York JFK to Israel started in March 1981 with a contract for 54 round-trip New York/Tel Aviv tours organised by the Tower Travel Corporation of New York. Other destinations, such as Athens, followed in April 1981, and were run by Homeric Tours of New York, operating once weekly throughout that summer. The Metro International operations, coupled with increased MAC passenger business, pushed Flying Tigers flight attendant ranks to their highest level – more than 300. Pictured above, passengers are seen disembarking from N748TA at Athens at the end of flight #3704 from New York JFK. Gabe Palmer, Palmer/Gabe, Inc.

747 Zurich-Charlotte service. Flying Tigers inaugurated a weekly scheduled air cargo service from Zurich, Switzerland, to Charlotte, N.C on April 5, 1981. The arrival of the airline's 747 also marked the first landing of a scheduled widebody at Charlotte's Douglas Municipal Airport. Its 214,000lbs of cargo comprised textiles, pharmaceuticals, apparel and printing products from European shippers. The new flight provided Swiss and other companies with valuable direct access to a gateway city in America's growing sunbelt.

Solar Challenge. The Solar Challenger, the world's only sun-powered aircraft, was loaded on board Flying Tigers 747-249F N808FT "William E. Bartling" at Los Angeles in 1981 for shipment to Paris. Following its display at the Paris Air Show between June 5 and 14, the ultralight aircraft, powered by a 2 ½ horsepower motor, with electricity synthesised by 16,128 photovoltaic cells, completed the 163-mile flight from Pontoise - Cormeilles Aerodrome, north of Paris to Manston in the UK, on July 7. It stayed aloft for 5 hours and 23 minutes, with pilot Stephen Ptacek at the controls, matching the accomplishment of its sister ship, the "Gossamer Albatross", which crossed the English Channel under human power in June 1979.

Fast trip. Flying Tigers transported the British designed and built record-breaking car, Thrust 2, to the United States for its world land speed record attempt. Propelled by a Rolls-Royce Avon turbojet engine, the 27-foot long car was airlifted from London Heathrow on a 747-200F to Los Angeles. It was on its way to the Bonneville Salt Flats in Utah in a bid to surpass the world land speed record of 622.407 miles per hour held for the past decade by American Gary Gabelich. Richard Noble broke Gary's record when he took Thrust 2 to a speed of 633.468 mph (1019.47 km/h) over one mile in the Black Rock Desert in Nevada on October 4, 1983.

TigerAir Boeing 707-138B. This particular Boeing 707-138B, has had a very busy and at times illustrious history. Purchased by TigerAir on October 19, 1978, it was the first of seven 707-138s ordered by Qantas Empire Airways Ltd in 1958. Initially named 'City of Canberra', it later became 'City of Melbourne'. In 1961 it was converted to a 707-138B and fitted with Pratt & Whitney JT3D-1 engines – it was also given the distinctive V-Jet livery in the same year. Sold to Pacific Western Airlines in 1967, it eventually joined TigerAir's fleet in 1978 receiving the registration N138TA, as well as undergoing a 33-passenger executive interior conversion. It was then sold to Airmark Corporation in 1983 and re-registered as N220AM the following year. Grounded in 1985 due to noise regulations, the aircraft was purchased by Community Transport (Comtran) for FAA certification. Subsequent ownership transfers led to its use by the Royal Embassy of Saudi Arabia. Having been placed in open storage at Southend, England in 1999, the aircraft was acquired by the Qantas Foundation Memorial seven years later, becoming VH-XBA and embarking on a ferry flight to Australia. Its last flight, on June 10, 2007, was to the Qantas Founders Outback Museum in Longreach where, as 707-138B, it remains on public display boasting an impressive flying record of 61,909 hours and 23,618 cycles. The picture above shows TigerAir's Boeing 707-138B N138TA at Basel in July 1981. Jacques Guillem Collection

Flying Tigers reunion. July 3, 1981, marked a special day for veterans of the renowned Flying Tigers (American Volunteer Group). Assembled at Oxnard Airport, 50 miles northwest of Los Angeles, they were treated to a close encounter with a symbol of their historic past – a meticulously restored Curtiss P-40 fighter. The aircraft executed several low-level passes over the field, eventually landing and taxiing over to the eagerly awaiting group. This event was part of the 40th AVG/CNAC (China National Aviation Corporation) reunion, bringing together pilots and ground crews who had served under General Claire Lee Chennault. The P-40 which was used in the making of the 1970 war film "Tora, Tora, Tora" was restored and given updated avionics by the TigerAir Service Center at Burbank Airport where the aircraft is based. During the day, the surviving veterans autographed the Warhawk and among the signatories were Robert "Duke" Hedman, H.C. "Link" Laughlin, R.J. "Catfish" Raine and Dick Rossi, who, post-war, were key players with Robert W. Prescott in founding The Flying Tiger Line.

Tigers' 747 in Frankfurt. Tilting up its nose, Flying Tigers 747-249F N807FT "Thomas Haywood" is seen in 1981 being loaded with heavy machinery cargo at the Tigers' terminal in Frankfurt, Germany.

First flight. Official training in the new 747 simulator began on July 24, 1981. The first crew members to get a taste of the sophisticated new equipment were: pictured below left and from the left, Captain Dick Wilson, Captain Karl Krout and Second Officer John Stolkin. The $6 million simulator was housed in a two-and-a-half-storey bay within the training centre (above left), perched on six hydraulic legs. Manufactured by the Link-Miles division of the Singer Company in Lancing, Sussex, England, the new simulator, the largest Comat (referring to Company Materials) in Flying Tigers' history, was broken down into 52 boxes occupying 14 pallet positions. It began its journey from London Heathrow on January 9, 1981, aboard Flying Tigers 747-249F N808FT "William E. Bartling", travelling via Paris Charles de Gaulle and New York JFK en route to Los Angeles. The delivery took place at the flight training centre located at the World Headquarters in LAX on January 12.

Wings from U.S. to U.K. From 1981, Flying Tigers played a part in the introduction of a new British Aerospace aircraft, the BAe 146, a 100-seat, four-engine jet. The wing structures were produced in Nashville, Tennessee, by Avco Aerostructures, Inc and Flying Tigers played a crucial role in transporting them to England. The wings, measuring 44 feet long by 10 feet wide, required careful handling. The structures were transported to New York, flown to London Heathrow and then trucked to the British Aerospace Factory in Hatfield. Flying Tigers transported one wing per month and increased that to three per month from 1982. The BBC television programme Nationwide regularly featured the development of the new aircraft, and Flying Tigers' involvement was highlighted on the show, providing valuable publicity. From the left, Doyle Brown, shipping manager Avco in Nashville; Bob Rizzo, regional manager Flying Tigers in Dallas-Fort Worth and Jim Gaines of Nashville forwarding company Air Compak.

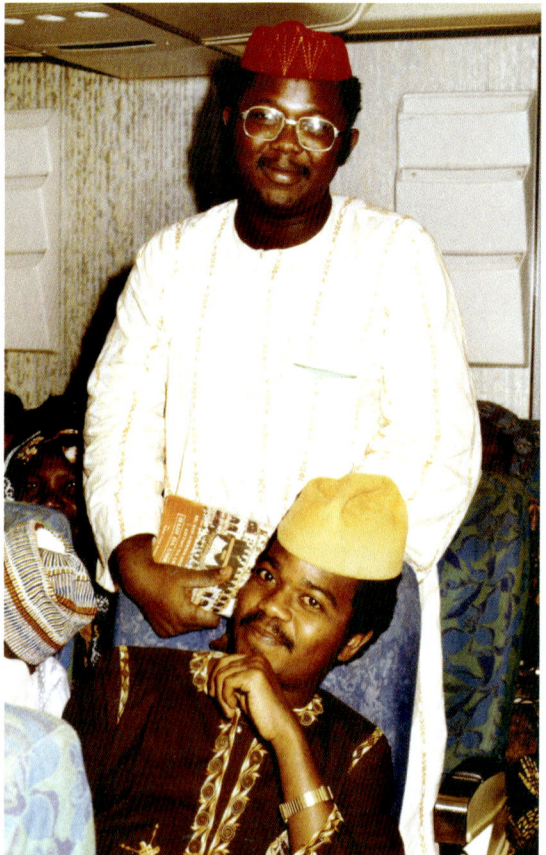

Hajj glimpses. Between September and November 1981 flight attendant Darryl May, captured these images during the Flying Tigers Hajj operation between Kano, Nigeria and Jeddah, Saudi Arabia on behalf of Trans Air Services. Darryl and 43 other flight attendants, mechanics and ground personnel were based in Kano to facilitate the airline's ten-week 747 Hajj contract carrying pilgrims to and from the holy city of Mecca. The flight attendant on the right photo is Dennis Ferrero.   Darryl J. May

Flight attendant Debbie McCoy with a passenger on a Hajj flight to Saudi Arabia, operated by a Flying Tigers 747.

Captain Starr Thompson

Crew corner

Captain Charles R. Clarke, Flight Engineer, Harold "Tippy" Ferrera and First Officer David O. Hill were at the controls of 747-132F N805FT bound for New York JFK from Frankfurt via Milan Malpensa in February 1981.

Captain Arvel Rector in the cockpit of a Tiger 747 on his last flight for the airline in July 1981.

First Officer Jean-Claude Démirdjian in the cockpit of a stretched DC-8.

The handling of Tiger 747 flight 05 on October 22, 1981, broke from the usual routine in Zurich, Switzerland, as orchestrated by the operations staff. Captain Martin Salva, a Seaboard captain hired in March 1955, took command of the aircraft at Zurich, his last trip before retiring. Manager Bob Widmer, on behalf of all Swiss Flying Tigers Operations, bid farewell to Captain Salva and presented him with a parting gift – a colourful Swiss cowbell.

Sweetening the deal. In the rapidly expanding American corn syrup sweetener market, innovation took centre stage, and Flying Tigers helped play a part in its advancement. In late 1981, British firm Tate and Lyle Process Technology (PROTECH), secured approval from the U.S. Food and Drug Administration to use its Taloflote method in processing corn syrups and subsequently, Taloflote corn syrup clarification plants were constructed at two U.S. locations. Meanwhile, a mobile Taloflote pilot plant, leased to another U.S. corn industry leader, was built in London and transported to the U.S. via Flying Tigers. In the image above, the pilot plant is being loaded onto a 747 at London Heathrow for transportation to the U.S.

Pressing a case for airfreight. The value of airfreight came into its own when MAN Roland, the largest German manufacturer of offset printing presses, delivered a 36-ton machine to Consolidated Trade Press of Philadelphia via Flying Tigers. Placed on eight pallets, the shipment occupied a third of the 747-249F N807FT "Thomas Haywood" on its way to the U.S. from Frankfurt, Germany. Airfreight saved three to four weeks in delivery time, with the nominally higher cost over ocean transport was fully justified by the freight's high value and demand in the U.S. MAN Roland, which manufactured in Offenbach outside Frankfurt, exported 75% of its production to more than 100 countries.

Narita gateway. Three Boeing 747 freighters lined up at the Flying Tigers' airfreight terminal at Tokyo Narita, Japan underscores the airline's strong presence in Asia. The distinctive orange and white striped light standards identify the Narita facility, where all Flying Tigers' scheduled flights transit between the U. S. and Asia. Captain Bob Martin

First Flight for "Quiet" DC-8. N787FT, the first Flying Tigers DC-8 to be re-engined with the new General Electric CFM56 powerplants, made its maiden test flight on March 4, 1982 from the McDonnell Douglas facility in Tulsa, Oklahoma, where the installation had taken place. On March 5, it was flown to Yuma, Arizona, for certification flying until late April. Despite being originally scheduled for delivery in August 1982, the first DC-8-73 was never handed over to Flying Tigers. Instead, as part of an effort to resize the Tigers fleet, four DC-8-73 stretched aircraft, including N787FT, were sold to United Parcel Service (UPS) for $80 million. All four, including #784, #786 and #788, were delivered to UPS by June 1983, with N787FT arriving in December 1982. The above shows N787FT during a flight test over the desert following conversion. McDonnell Douglas

Metro's Scheduled to Brussels. Founded as a passenger charter carrier in December 1980 by Flying Tigers, Metro International Airways took off on March 25, 1981 on its first low-cost twice-a-week scheduled 747 rotation operated from New York to Brussels, Belgium. Flight 30 departed New York's John F. Kennedy International Airport on Thursdays and Sundays at 8:30 p.m., arriving at Brussels International Airport at 9:15 a.m. the following day. Flight 31 left the Belgian capital at 12:30 p.m. on Mondays and Fridays, reaching New York at 1:30 p.m. the same day. The new U.S./Europe schedules introduced three classes of service – Economy, Metropolitan Class and Captain's Deck. While maintaining passenger charter flights to Europe, the Middle East, the Caribbean and Hawaii, Metro emerged as the sole U.S. carrier providing widebody 747 service to Brussels. Fares from New York ranged from $239 to $524 one-way and from $479 to $945 round-trip. In addition to the U.S.-to-Europe rotation, Metro began two scheduled 747 flights services per week between New York and Tel Aviv on October 31, 1982, after obtaining authorisations from both U.S. and Israeli authorities. An intermediate stop was made at Brussels, and the airline also held the right to carry airfreight and passengers between Brussels and Tel Aviv. The photo above captures Metro International Boeing 747-212B N748TA at Brussels in April 1982.

Guy Viselé

Metro's "really going places" – as bag tags proclaimed – with its new scheduled service between the U.S. and Belgium.

Metro boarding passes, above, are in red, white or blue depending on Economy, Captain's Deck or Metropolitan class.

The Metro 747s were previously operated by Singapore Airlines, with the upper deck designed as a First Class lounge. Metro's upper deck was known as the Captain's Deck, and boasted 16 extra-wide seats. The distinctive metal artwork on the rear bulkhead, originating from Singapore Airlines, was preserved, as were the rear "berthable divans" or "slumberettes", discreetly separated by a curtain from the last row of seats. Passengers were intrigued by the sculpted metal wall, which depicted the founding of Singapore and prominently featured the imposing figure of Sir Stamford Raffles.

Fuel conservation. Amid the first oil price crisis of 1973-74, kerosene costs nearly doubled within a year. By the peak of the second oil price crisis in May 1981, they skyrocketed to nearly ten times the 1973 baseline. Responding to this surge, Flying Tigers initiated a fuel conservation campaign displaying posters throughout its network. From April 1981, the left-hand poster, aimed at fostering company-wide awareness about escalating fuel prices, encouraged employee contributions to conservation efforts. The right-hand poster introduced a reduced engine taxi procedure in a bid to enhance fuel efficiency. Projections indicated that in 1982, Flying Tigers aircraft would spend 11,500 hours taxiing, with a four-engine DC-8 taxi consuming 700 gallons/hour and up to 1,100 gallons/hour for the 747. This equated to over 10 million gallons of taxi fuel. Achieving a modest reduction of less than 20% in fuel consumption translated to savings exceeding $2 million.

Ocean Venture Deployment. Members of the 372nd Transportation, 101st Airborne Division, disembarked Flying Tigers 747-249F N806FT "Robert W. Prescott" during Exercise Ocean Venture '82 at the Roosevelt Roads Naval Station, Puerto Rico on April 25, 1982.
U.S. National Archives, Technical Sergeant Frank Garzelnick

Lockheed demonstration. On April 16, 1982, Lockheed-Georgia Company representatives visited Flying Tigers' headquarters to showcase the Lockheed L-100-30 Hercules and its potential for short-haul routes. The four-engine turboprop underwent a test flight for management and was subsequently parked in front of the maintenance hangars for two days. N4170M served as Lockheed's demonstrator from June 1981 until its delivery to Líneas Aéreas del Estado (LADE) on December 10, 1982.

Cub onboard. A three-week-old lioness from Dallas/Fort Worth was taken via a Flying Tigers DC-8-63 to the Southern California Wildlife Waystation in Los Angeles in May 1982. The flight crew, consisting of First Officer John Tymczyszyn (left), Captain Frank Therian (centre) and Second Officer Charles Rogers (right), took a personal interest in the unique "cargo". With just the three of them onboard, John, being comfortable with cats, assumed the responsibility of feeding the cub with a baby bottle during the flight. The cub's playful antics led to a moment of tension when it jumped out of John's arms and headed toward the controls. This caused some consternation when, approaching Los Angeles International Airport, the crew had to explain that they were facing a potential delay because a lion was blocking the rudder pedals. Fortunately, they successfully coaxed the lioness back into her cage just in time for the descent. Reflecting on the experience, John wondered if the cub's escape was triggered by hearing the term "Tiger" on the radio.

Captain Bob Martin

Leasing to Pacific East Air. Established in 1981 by former Western Airlines employees, primarily to serve the Los Angeles to Honolulu route, Pacific East Air swiftly took to the skies as a new scheduled U.S. passenger airline. It began operations after securing a lease for a passenger-configured Flying Tigers DC-8-63CF in June 1982. The specific aircraft, N797FT, donned a distinctive blue and gold Pacific East Air livery. In August 1982, Flying Tigers further contributed to Pacific East Air's fleet by delivering DC-8-61CF N867FT. The above photographs of the two aircraft were taken at Los Angeles in December 1982.

Jacques Guillem Collection

Thanks for the lift. Flying Tigers Captain John Franzone received an affectionate greeting from a grateful 1,200lb sea walrus upon arrival in Cleveland, Ohio, from Orlando, Florida in June 1981. The walrus was part of a Flying Tigers charter for SeaWorld marine amusement parks which involved transporting a diverse array of performing whales, porpoises, sea mammals and other animals from SeaWorld in San Diego, California, to the Orlando park and subsequently to the Cleveland facility. The DC-8 charter crew included Captain Franzone, First Officer Rich Van Veen and Second Officer Dean Wolfe, with Rolf Ellefson as the maintenance representative.   First Officer Rich Van Veen

Simple shape – complex challenge. Flying Tigers transported two steel rings, each measuring 141 inches in diameter and weighing a hefty 19,603lbs, from Paris, France to St. Louis, Missouri, on behalf of Nooter Company in Lyon, France in 1982. Securing the oversized sections inside the aircraft proved challenging for the team at Charles de Gaulle Airport. CDG terminal personnel Carmelo Ciaramella and Daniel Martini collaborated on the project with Dick Feuerherm, senior planner for cargo handling equipment and Ian Jackson, Senior Director of traffic services. Through their joint efforts, the ground staff were able to prepare the rings for shipment by designing a metal frame to hold them in place. The rings reached St. Louis without any incidents, thanks to the meticulous teamwork of the Flying Tigers team, including Daniel Martini, D. Miele, R. Bourges, P. Car, Carmelo Ciaramella and ramp personnel at CDG; Jean-Pierre Felix in Lyon; Juergen Heck in Frankfurt; H. Wilmoth in St. Louis; and Jackson and Feuerherm in Los Angeles.

Alain Chaille Archives

South America Here We Come. The Civil Aeronautics Board officially granted Flying Tigers the authority for all-cargo services between the United States, Brazil and Argentina on April 21, 1982. Following detailed planning, the inaugural scheduled jetfreighter flight to Brazil took off from Miami, Florida, shortly after midnight on July 31, 1982 destined for São Paulo. The flight, under the command of Captain Brian Esler (third from the top), carried over 46,000 pounds. The return flight had an increased payload of 62,500 revenue pounds. Present for this milestone at Miami were key figures, among them Pete Hubbard, Senior VP Marketing & Sales; Jack Kane, VP Sales System Accounts; Nissen Davis, VP Public Relations & Advertising; Hermann Spegel, VP Central Region; Carl Asmus, Director of Advertising; Vince Del Marco, District Sales Manager-Miami; Len Fronzak from Miami and representatives from Miami sales, customer service, maintenance and operations.

The Silver Ghost. Seventy-five years of Rolls-Royce manufacturing expertise, both airborne and earthbound, met on the tarmac at London Heathrow Airport in July 1982 when a 1907 Silver Ghost vintage car and two 1982 RB-211 engines were loaded on board Flying Tigers 747-132F, N804FT. The car, weighing nearly two tons, was being airfreighted to New York John F. Kennedy to appear during a two-month anniversary tour throughout the United States. The two RB-211s were being flown for Delta Air Lines, which uses the Rolls-Royce engines in its fleet of Lockheed L-1011 TriStar jets.

On the ground at JFK with the flight's crew, left to right: Second Officer Sandra Szigeti; First Officer Leslie E. "Les" Johnson (seated) and Captain John H. "Rocky" Orth. Once clearing the airport, the car, mounted on four wooden wheels and finished with genuine silver-plated fittings, was rushed to Central Park for a special appearance. The car, which moves at an average speed of 25 mph and covers just 12 miles to the gallon, was also seen at the Rolls-Royce Owner's Club annual meeting in Florida, before being flown by Flying Tigers to Los Angeles.

Farewell: Crew Retirements

After 32 years of service with Flying Tigers, Captain John "Jack" Bliss retired in September 1982 following his last flight on a Boeing 747. The photo shows Jack Bliss with his daughter Kristianne "Kristi" Bliss Peake after a passenger charter flight.

Captain Carlyle R. "Carl" Hirschberg with flight attendant Pat Parlette. Carl joined Seaboard & Western on May 10, 1950. He was appointed chief pilot with Seaboard World in June 1965 and vice president of flight in September 1969, a position he held until October 1980 when he returned to his first love, flying as captain on the 747. Carl retired on July 9, 1982

After 32 years of service with Flying Tigers, Captain Starr K. Thompson retired in September 1982, his last flight was on a 747. He was hired by the Flying Tiger Line on July 24, 1950, five days later than Captain Jack Bliss.

Mr. Pasquale's transatlantic tale. In July 1956, Mr. Pasquale set out from Italy for a new life in the United States as a passenger on the ocean liner "Andre Doria". Sadly the vessel, bound for New York City, sank while approaching the coast of Nantucket, Massachusetts on July 26, after colliding with the MS "Stockholm", claiming 46 of the 1,706 passengers and crew on board. Mr. Pasquale, 70 years old when this picture was taken in November 1982 and a resident of the Bronx, New York, made his first trip back home since that fateful night, and this time chose a less traumatic means of travel – a Metro International Airways 747-200 charter flight to Rome. Standing, left to right, Tandrea Lockhart, Linda Lutz, David Lusk and Tony Maglimont; and seated, left to right, Chris Zanella, Pasquale and Sharon Way.

Flight Attendant Keri Clark

Race in Macau. Marking eight years in a row, Flying Tigers took part in the prestigious Macau Grand Prix in November 1982. Since 1978, the airline had not only entered but also co-sponsored the race. In the photo above, Lee Mitchell, Flying Tigers' Senior Director of Information Systems, is seen competing in the Macau Guia Race with his Porsche 924. As in the previous year, he secured a first-place finish, relishing the attention befitting winners. The event, attended by over 50,000 racing enthusiasts, including cargo agents, customers and friends of Flying Tigers, served as an outstanding platform to showcase and promote the airline.

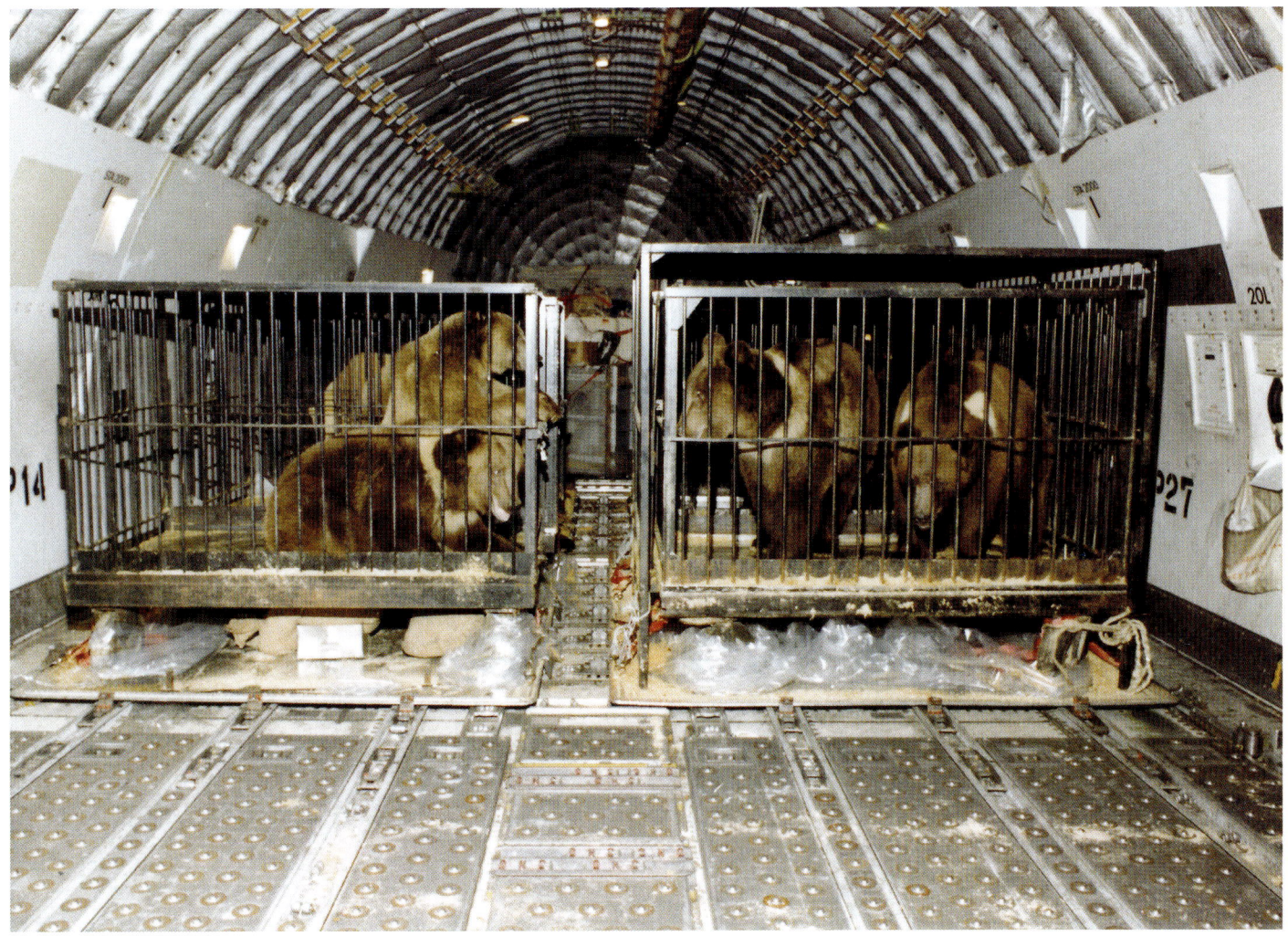

Circus to Los Angeles. The circus visited Flying Tigers' Los Angeles terminal for an exclusive two-night event in December 1982. The first night featured 12 bears, including 5 polar bears, plus 17 tigers and 16 baboons. Three performing Indian elephants captivated terminal personnel and television news cameras on the second night. The animals were en route to Tokyo via Flying Tigers 747 for a month-long engagement organised by Kaye Enterprises of Hollywood, California to appear at the Korakuen Great American Circus. They travelled on separate nights owing to the elephants and bears not getting along.   Brett Fish

Crew Corner

Captain Bob Martin's final flight took him through Honolulu where he was garlanded with a neck-full of leis.

Captain Raymond J. "Ray" Poole, a former Seaboard World pilot hired in 1950, enjoys some of the retirement cake presented to him on his last flight at New York Kennedy Airport in late 1982. Helen Hoating, flight department at JFK

October 1983 at Tel Aviv, standing in front of N601BN are, from left: flight attendant Kenneth Barton, a TLV airport cabin cleaner, flight attendants Treso Koken, Donna Sheehan and Randy Brooks. Kenneth Barton Collection

Aircraft swap with Pan Am. In December 1982, Flying Tigers and Pan American World Airways announced an agreement to swap four Pan Am 747-100 freighters (N654PA, 658, 771 and 901) for three Flying Tigers 747-212B passenger aircraft (N747FT, 748 and 749.) The exchange officially took effect on February 24, 1983. The newly acquired freighters were seamlessly integrated into Flying Tigers' fleet, which consisted of thirteen 747 freighters (ten 200s and three 100s) and 26 DC-8-60s. The deal enabled Flying Tigers to focus its resources on its cargo business while still meeting charter and military contract commitments using leased aircraft. Metro International passenger flights were then operated with former Braniff 747-127 N601BN. The acquisition of the four Pan Am freighters not only increased frequency and capacity to Europe but also facilitated the replacement of DC-8s with 747s on scheduled routes to South America. Additionally, it allowed Flying Tigers to extend its services to the Middle East and Australia. Above is Flying Tigers 747-121F N771PA taxiing at Hong Kong Kai Tak Airport in May 1983. The aircraft was re-registered N819FT in July 1983.

Largest flying cowshed in the world. The most extensive single airlift of pure-bred pedigree cattle to the United Kingdom took place on April 12, 1983. Flying Tigers' 747-245F N811FT, named "Houston Rehrig", flew 157 Holstein heifers and 7 bulls from Canada to Prestwick, Scotland. These prized cattle, valued at over a quarter of a million pounds, were destined to enhance existing herds and traditional dairy breeds on British and Scottish farms. After spending two months in quarantine in Canada, they underwent a twelve-hour flight to Prestwick. Once transferred from the freighter to a lairage near Prestwick Airport, Captain Robert H. "Bob" Poindexter, who led the flight, remarked, "The animals adapted very quickly to their new surroundings in the aircraft. They were better passengers than some human beings, a lot less trouble."

APS Air Publicity Services Ltd

Expertise with outsized cargo. In July 1983, the London Heathrow team at Flying Tigers showcased top teamwork by efficiently managing the handling of two full 747 charter loads from London to Edmonton, Alberta, Canada. These shipments carried the entire contents of a furnace, originating from the Midlands area. The cargo included bundles of 46-foot pipes, and ably illustrated the airline's commitment and logistical expertise.

New MAC passenger plane. Flying Tigers began its 1983-84 Military Airlift Command (MAC) passenger and cargo operations to destinations in Asia, Europe and the U.S. on October 1, 1983. For the task, the airline leased a 747-287B passenger jet from Aerolíneas Argentinas, LV-MLO "889" (though the N889FT registration was never officially adopted). Flying Tigers revamped the cabin interior, including new carpeting, and increased the seating capacity from 350 to 470. The various adjustments amounted to 7,500 man-hours for maintenance and 850 man-hours for engineering within a five-week timeframe. Prior to the inaugural flight, informal dedication ceremonies and walk-through events took place in the Flying Tigers hangar at its HQ. Eddy J. Gual

A large number of personnel were instrumental in securing and preparing aircraft 889 for MAC service, from left: D. Falvey, manager inventory planning; M. Edwards, facilities & equipment (F&E) mechanic; Don Nielsen, flightline shift manager; R. Hatcher, F&E mechanic; J. Toro and T. Moore, maintenance supervisors; mechanics K. Kelly and E. Comacho, sheet metal (SM), J. Caceres, F&E N. Daniels, H. Bergman and E. Larson, SM; M. Harris, F&E lead mechanic; R. Hawn, SM lead mechanic; mechanics R. Clayton and V. Le, SM, D. Warner, F&E, E. Paliungas, SM, and B. Bonnell, F&E; J. Butts, material planner; M. Kealy, F&E lead mechanic; R. Fleming and R. Young, F&E mechanics; and R. Wier, maintenance supervisor.

Marge Hough, director of passenger service, second from right, dedicates new MAC aircraft with champagne aided by, left to right, Louise Keenan and Betty Carver, passenger service; Oakley Smith, director of flight training and standards; and Harold Woody, vice-president technical operations.

Chairman Wayne Hoffman, on the right, toured the aircraft and greeted flight attendants, namely Houston Wray, Marilyn McCaig and Betty Carver, from left to right.

Close call in Frankfurt. Bound for Frankfurt and Amsterdam, Flying Tigers 4006/08, 747-249F N806FT "Robert W. Prescott", took off from New York JFK on October 10, 1983 with Captain R. Burson, First Officer W. Galloway, Second Officer K. Halls, 15 passengers and pallets of mixed cargo on board. After landing in Frankfurt on October 11, unloading began. Due to a shift change and absent shift supervisor, two Italian workers continued the task. The pallets, though identified by handwritten instructions, didn't have the prescribed Offload Control Sheet and two were mistakenly left in the upper cargo compartment. The pressure was on for flight 9014/11 to depart for Amsterdam as the second officer was trying to direct non-English-speaking workers. Once ready, the aircraft left the parking area and taxied to runway 25R with the same flight crew on board, three passengers and the two pallets of cargo. During the take-off roll at 0805z, between fifty and sixty knots, a detached pallet shifted and caused a pitch-up, followed by a nose-down motion. The crew attempted to use wheel braking but unable to stop, they steered off the runway, resulting in substantial damage. The aircraft came to a rest in a nose-up position between the runways. There were no injuries. The probable causes cited included movement of the insecurely restrained pallet, time constraints, inadequate supervision, procedural lapses and communication challenges.

Victory flight for Thrust 2. The jet-propelled Thrust 2 car that clinched the World Land Speed Record for Britain at Black Rock Desert in Nevada on October 4, 1983, returned to London Heathrow on board Flying Tigers 747-249FT N810FT. The car, achieving a record speed of 633.468 mph, was driven by British businessman Richard Noble, making him the fastest man on wheels since American Gary Gabelich secured the title for the U.S. in 1970. Noble was at Heathrow to receive his 8,000lbs championship car. This marked "third time lucky" for both Noble and Flying Tigers, as the airline had transported the car from Heathrow to the U.S. and back on all three occasions since 1981 when the first attempt was made to secure the record for Britain.

From Metro to Tower. The agreement to swap Metro International's 747-200s for Pan Am 747-100Fs came as a shock to Metro's dedicated crews, particularly those who had relocated from the West Coast to New York. Despite the exchange, Flying Tigers, Metro's parent company, opted to continue passenger operations by leasing a well-worn 1971-built 747 from Braniff, known as the Big Orange N601BN. The leased 747 enabled Metro to maintain schedules between New York, Brussels and Tel Aviv. However, without warning, Flying Tigers abruptly announced Metro's shutdown, leading to the airline's last flight on October 29, 1983, after nearly three years of operation. Following Metro's closure, Morris K. Nachtomi acquired the "Tower" brand from a package tour agency called Tower Travel Corporation, leasing the former Metro 747 to continue the New York-Brussels-Tel Aviv route. Rebranded as Tower Air, the stickers hastily applied over Metro's titles began peeling during transatlantic flights, leaving the aircraft looking rather shabby. Despite the cosmetic issues (as seen in the above picture taken in Brussels), Tower Air quickly shifted focus to international charter flights, particularly to Israel.

Kenneth Barton

Braniff's colourful 747. The former Big Orange Braniff N601BN held the record for the highest mileage among American 747s, flying the Dallas-Honolulu route daily for over a decade. Braniff's distinctive leather seats were coloured differently in each of the five main deck zones. E zone's patina was tobacco-themed.

Kenneth Barton

Positive rate, gear up! Boeing 747-249F N808FT, named "William E. Bartling," after taking off from London Heathrow in November 1983.
Richard Vandervord

Impressive dimensions. John Rovello, Flying Tigers' Director of Terminal Services at JFK International Airport, provided this snow-covered view of the airline's expansive freight facility. Covering 36 acres, it offered over 300,000 square feet of warehouse, office and maintenance space. Centre left, behind the 747, is Building 262 which handled domestic and export traffic globally, and boasted 62,000 square feet of warehouse space. Above, Hangar 6 managed import traffic with 75,000 square feet of warehouse space. On average, the facility processed 4,800 shipments a week, serving 1,270 trucks and handling 5,300,000lbs of freight.

First Flying Tigers 727 on line. Between June and December 1983, Flying Tigers operated two Boeing 727-100 "quick change" freighters, N496WC and N498WC, leased from Wien Air Alaska on routes connecting New Orleans, Memphis, Chicago and Kansas City, St. Louis, Chicago. In January 1984, the airline added its first of seven 727s leased from Aviation Sales Company Inc. This aircraft, N1929, a former American Airlines passenger jet, was converted to cargo configuration at Monarch Aviation in Miami, Florida. On January 17, it began service on the Kansas City, St. Louis, Chicago route, with Captain William P. "Bill" Smith, First Officer Alan G. "Al" Samford and Second Officer William C. Harvey at the helm. The remaining six examples, all former AA 727-100 aircraft, were similarly converted and delivered to Flying Tigers by August 1984. In September 1984, N1929 was re-registered as N930FT.

Jacques Guillem Collection

100 Down Under. A significant milestone was achieved on March 13, 1984 when Flying Tigers completed its 100th charter load of computer products, transporting them in a DC-8-63CF from Los Angeles to Sydney, Australia on behalf of Digital Equipment Corporation. Within days, another Flying Tigers 747 jet freighter arrived with an even larger consignment of Digital's products.

Burson-Marsteller

Meeting demand. In November 1983, N748WA, a leased 747-273C convertible freighter from World Airways, provided Flying Tigers with the flexibility to adapt its fleet for cargo or passenger business, depending on demand. It was then decided to convert the aircraft from passenger configuration to cargo in April 1984. Flying Tigers' maintenance personnel at the Los Angeles headquarters carried out the work, and the aircraft began service on Military Airlift Command freight flights on May 1.

Jacques Guillem Collection

Shamu Express. Flying Tigers operated its first 747 charter flight for SeaWorld amusement parks on April 30, 1984. The Shamu Express, 747-245F N811FT, carried the famous 4,000lb performing killer whale, Shamu, along with Namu, a female counterpart, two beluga whales, ten dolphins, six penguins and a Malaysian sea otter from San Diego, California, to Cleveland, Ohio. The "passengers" were en route from their winter residence in San Diego to SeaWorld's park in Aurora, Ohio, for the summer. The airline had been transporting SeaWorld animals in DC-8s since 1974, but the killer whales had now outgrown the type. Dick Feuerherm, senior planner of cargo handling equipment, collaborated closely with SeaWorld for months to develop bigger containers and procedures for the move. Captain Charles L. "Chuck" Cumiford, First Officer Trevor R. Lewis and Second Officer Richard D. "Rick" MacGibbon piloted the 747 during the delicate operation, with Cameron Forbes, maintenance representative, overseeing the loading process from Los Angeles to San Diego.

DC-8 returns. In April 1984, N862FT, a DC-8-61CF that had been subleased to Emery Worldwide, was returned to Flying Tigers. The aircraft was brought back to bolster capacity for the remainder of 1984 and officially re-entered service with the airline on April 30. Frank de Koster

The Super 62. A solitary DC-8-62, a leased -62CF with registration N3931A, was operated by Flying Tigers from June to December 1984 providing additional capacity on domestic routes later served by 727s. Captured at the headquarters maintenance hangar in Los Angeles in June 1984, the aircraft had retained its distinctive Alitalia livery. Tiger's pilots flew this particular aircraft during its time in service.

Headquarters Open House. Around 800 headquarters and Los Angeles terminal employees, along with their families and friends, explored the facilities at Flying Tigers' headquarters on June 2, 1984. The showcased aircraft featured the passenger jets 747-287B LV-MLO and 727-23F N1932 on the left, alongside DC-8-63CF N781FT. Standing proudly on the right was 747-249F N806FT "Robert W. Prescott". In addition, visitors were able to view Tiger International's restored Curtiss P-40E N40FT also named in honour of the Flying Tiger Line's founder.

Second 747 flight starts down under. A second weekly scheduled service, flight #77, from the United States to Australia was inaugurated by Flying Tigers on Wednesday, July 11, 1984. The 747 freighter took off from Los Angeles at 8 p.m. on Wednesday, making a stop in Honolulu and arriving in Sydney at 7:30 a.m. on Friday, July 13. The southbound scheduled U.S.-Australia rotation, which was started in September 1983, featured a Saturday departure from Los Angeles and a Monday arrival in Sydney and Melbourne. The captivating photograph above shows 747-249F "William E. Bartling" soaring over Sydney's iconic landmarks, the Harbour Bridge and Opera House. Taken by renowned Australian aerial photographer Ron Israel from a single-engine light aircraft, the shot captures Captain Oakley M. Smith, First Officer Marvin J. "Marv" Griffith and Second Officer John C. Grago at the controls of the 747 en route from Sydney to Melbourne. Meticulous planning between the Tiger crew and the pilot of the chase aircraft, with cooperation from Sydney aviation officials facilitated this remarkable image for use in various publicity and promotional material.

Ron Israel

Olympic Cargo. Flying Tigers transported plane loads of Olympic-related cargo for the 1984 summer games in Los Angeles. This included numerous horses, dozens of rowing boats, sailboats, various athletic gear and machinery essential for supporting the games. The image captures a moment on July 5, 1984, when rowing boats intended for Olympic competition at Lake Casitas in Ojai, California, were being carefully offloaded from the 747-245F N815FT "W. Henry Renninger" at Los Angeles.

The last DC-8-63 to leave LAX. Marking the end of an era, Flying Tigers DC-8-63AF N783FT taxied out from Los Angeles International Airport on September 23, 1984, en route to Atlanta, Georgia to be re-engined by Cammacorp before being acquired by German Cargo. This was the last DC-8-63 of the airline's original DC-8 fleet, which it had flown since 1968. By the end of 1984, several DC-8-61s and one DC-8-62 series example that were still in domestic service, had been phased out. The image above is of N783FT, photographed by Maintenance Contracts Administrator Halli Gudmundsson, as it taxied out from Tigers' maintenance facility. Below, N783FT is seen in Atlanta in October 1984 after being converted to -73AF with new CFM56-2 high-bypass turbofan engines, in a photo provided by Eddy J. Gual.

Leased 747 for MAC business. From October 1984 to May 1987, Flying Tigers leased a 747-273C from World Airways enabling it to capitalise on revenue opportunities related to the expansion of Military Airlift Command business. The aircraft, N749WA, was operated and maintained by Flying Tigers personnel throughout the lease period. Initially intended for three months, the lease was extended until May 1987 when the aircraft was returned to World Airways. Above is N749WA in San Francisco in November 1985, still adorned in its former VIAZA basic colour scheme. Thomas Robert Singfield Collection

Crew corner

Upon his retirement, Captain Ralph Mitchell, who held the fifth position on the pilot seniority list, had amassed 33 years with Flying Tigers. He marked the occasion with an "around the world" flight that concluded in San Francisco on March 17, 1984. Throughout his extensive career, Ralph piloted a variety of aircraft, including DC-6s, DC-6As, Lockheed L-1049H Constellations, 707s, DC-8s and 747s. Before joining the airline, he had flown with the China National Aviation Corporation (CNAC) in China.

Captain Oakley M. Smith, Jr., completed his final flight as the airline's most senior active captain on September 24, 1984, having joined the Tigers in 1950. In addition to his responsibilities as a line captain, he had held various supervisory roles throughout his distinguished career, such as check pilot, chief pilot in Newark, JFK and Detroit, director of flight training and senior director of flight operations. His sister Barbara was among those who welcomed Oakley on his last flight.

After 29 years of service with Flying Tigers, Captain Paul H. Crowley arrived at LAX on September 25, 1984, marking his final flight. He was accompanied by fellow crew members Angelo J. "Angie" Regina on the right and Michael D. Johann in the centre.

Final DC-8 flight. Douglas DC-8-61CF N867FT (seen above in Los Angeles) was the airline's last DC-8. Having joined the fleet in 1977, the aircraft had logged 44,995 flight hours and 16,079 cycles by the time it landed in Atlanta, Georgia, on December 31, 1984, as flight #543. The event, which marked the conclusion of a sixteen-year era for Flying Tigers, was brought about by the enforcement of Federal noise regulations on January 1, 1985. Commanded by Captain Dick Andrews, with First Officer George Beck and Second Officer John Dill, the crew had transported 50,656lbs of cargo from San Juan, including pharmaceuticals, flashlights, lanterns and electrical equipment. After being unloaded in Atlanta, Captain Mike Johnsen, First Officer Thomas O'Connor and Second Officer William Gormly ferried the DC-8 to Pinal Air Park, Arizona. The aircraft was subsequently sold to United Parcel Services, re-registered as N703UP and equipped with CFM56 engines. Jacques Guillem Collection

Bound for Ethiopia. On January 14, 1985, Flying Tigers operated its first 747 relief flight to Ethiopia in collaboration with the aid organisation, Operation California. The 747, N810FT "Clifford G. Groh", destined for Addis Ababa, departed Los Angeles International Airport carrying 150,000lbs of medicines, medical equipment and housing materials to help victims of drought and famine. The flight made its first stop in New York John F. Kennedy Airport, where an additional 40,000lbs of relief goods were loaded, and then made a fuel stop in Frankfurt, Germany. The picture shows news media, relief organisation representatives and Flying Tigers personnel watching the big jet as it taxied out for takeoff on its first leg of the journey, with Captain John Dziubala, First Officer Russ Beltz and Second Officer Dan Deleuw in control. From JFK to Frankfurt, the crew included Captain Ralph Jarvis, First Officer Bob Douroux and Second Officer Bryan Ableidinger. At the helm for the historic landing at Addis Ababa were Captain Arthur John, First Officer Dennis Slavick and Second Officer Jim Harrigan.

Trinidad and Tobago. Flying Tigers established the sole U.S.-Trinidad and Tobago 747 all-cargo operation with an inaugural flight on January 23, 1985. The new service was added to the mid-week southbound flight #50, which operated weekly to Brazil and Argentina. There to witness the first arrival in Port-of-Spain, Trinidad were, from left to right: Captain Richard Hamm, First Officer Ed Bowen, General Manager Eusebio Cotto and Manager of Freight Services for Latin America Frank Algeciras.   Mark Taylor

Lifelift to Ethiopia. On January 29, 1985, Flying Tigers 747-245F N815FT, laden with 234,700lbs of relief goods, landed in Addis Ababa, Ethiopia, marking the culmination of a humanitarian effort conceived and executed by Flying Tigers employees throughout the airline's global network. Some of the Lifelift participants gathered for a photograph with Executive Vice President Lewis Jordan at New York John F. Kennedy Airport just before the airlift departed. Pictured above from left are: Steve Hanks, director of labour relations and chairman of the Employee Lifelift Committee; Michelle Rizza, a flight attendant accompanying the flight; Captain Randy Patterson; Lewis Jordan; First Officer Mick O'Connor; Captain Hal Ewing; Second Officer Charles Gallardo and First Officer Chuck Cozad.

Cyril Morris

Lifelift to Ethiopia

At the controls of N815FT from New York to Brussels were Captain Randy Patterson, First Officer Chuck Cozad and Second Officer Paul Zahner.

Veteran Los Angeles Times reporter Charles Hillinger, temporarily in the captain's seat, was onboard Lifelift to cover the event. Hillinger interviewed First Officer Chuck Cozad while the aircraft was cruising at 37,000 feet.

From Brussels to Addis Ababa, the crew included Captain Hal Ewing, First Officer Mick O'Connor and Second Officer Charles Gallardo.

On board the flight were volunteer flight attendants Michelle Rizza on the left and Becky Rasmussen, right.

Flying Tigers' 747-245F N815FT "W Henry Renninger" was photographed at Addis Ababa on January 29, 1985, with the crew standing on the stairs. The aircraft carried a vital load totalling 234,771lbs of medical supplies, food and clothing for the victims of Ethiopia's devastating famine. A notable feature was the red Flying Tigers Lifelift decal adorning the fuselage.

Charter Operations Representative Jochem Derschow (standing), who had boarded N815FT in Brussels, supervised the offloading process at Addis Ababa. The operation, which included retrieving Tiger-owned pallets, lasted approximately six and a half hours.

Ethiopian workers load relief goods from the aircraft onto trucks bound for the Adventist Development and Relief Agency warehouse.

The small airport featured an assortment of military and civilian aircraft, with an Interflug Tupolev Tu-134A visible in the background on the left, but none were as imposing as the massive 747. With the offloading completed, the aircraft departed for Sharjah, U.A.E., where the crew enjoyed a well-deserved rest.

Khartoum relief operation. Flying Tigers carried over 240,000lbs of relief supplies from New York to Khartoum, Sudan on March 6, 1985 marking the airline's third 747 aid flight to northern and eastern Africa within a six-week period. The Sudan airlift was conducted in collaboration with Americares, a private U.S. voluntary relief agency. The aircraft, 747-249F N807FT, was operated by volunteer Flying Tigers Captains Hal Ewing and Randy Patterson; First Officers Chuck Cozad and Mick O'Connor; and Second Officers Fred McClurkin and Paul Zahner, all providing their services on their days off at no cost. Flight attendants Sharrie Schleis and Kenneth Barton also volunteered their services to assist on the flight. The picture shows N807FT baking in the sun at Khartoum while refuelling and offloading were in progress.

Kenneth Barton

The operation coincided with the visit of U.S. Vice President George Bush (in the white shirt) and his wife Barbara (centre) who were in Khartoum as part of the relief efforts to help African famine victims. Vice President Bush greeted Flying Tigers and Americares personnel and watched supplies being unloaded from the aircraft. Kenneth Barton

New heights in heft. In March 1985, Flying Tigers set another record for transporting heavy, outsized cargo. The achievement involved moving a 40-ton hydroelectric plant core from London to Dubai in the United Arab Emirates. This was the heaviest single shipment ever transported from the UK aboard a Flying Tigers freighter and one of the heaviest single airfreight consignments to depart from London Heathrow. During the loading, the substantial 30-foot cargo necessitated the use of two cranes and a belly loader. It took more than 150 straps to secure the cargo inside the aircraft.

Ramp servicemen Ken Williams and Tony Quainton secured the valuable vehicle along with a number of tyres on board N749WA.

U.K.'s most valuable car. The Blue Train Bentley – the most valuable car ever sold in Britain – was transported by Flying Tigers 747-273C to a private collection in America during March 1985. The 1930s vehicle, crafted for one of the "Bentley Boys" Woolf Barnato, was carefully loaded on board N749WA at Heathrow Airport. Barnato, celebrated for three Le Mans victories, and who later became a Bentley Motors director, anonymously auctioned the Bentley at Sotheby's, fetching a five-figure sum. Famous for beating the Côte d'Azur Blue Train Express, the car arrived in London just four minutes before the train reached Calais (apparently this is based on folklore and didn't happen quite the way it was promoted at the time). Flying Tigers delivered the Bentley to its new owner in San Francisco. Palletised and ready for loading, the Blue Train Bentley above is being checked out, from the left by: John Rogers, ramp operations supervisor; Dave Thomas, lead ramp serviceman; and Bob Warner, duty manager.

USA for Africa. Teaming up with "USA for Africa" which had organised one of America's most high-profile relief efforts, Flying Tigers transported 231,463lbs of emergency supplies to Khartoum, Sudan and Addis Ababa, Ethiopia in June 1985. This was the sixth time a Flying Tigers 747 freighter had delivered aid to famine-stricken African nations, however it was the first airlift to be organised by the non-profit group made up of 45 top American recording artists. Proceeds from their hit record "We Are the World" and related merchandise sales were channelled to support the famine victims. The flight, which followed a Los Angeles-New York-Brussels-Khartoum-Addis Ababa route, gained considerable media attention worldwide. Such artists as Quincy Jones, Kenny Rogers, Harry Belafonte and Diana Ross went to Flying Tigers' facilities in Los Angeles, New York and Brussels, to witness the loading and departure. The flight, which included Marlon Jackson and USA for Africa president Kenneth Kragen, played a crutcial role in the humanitarian effort in Africa. Above right: Diana Ross toured the aircraft, N812FT, as additional freight was loaded on board. Below right: On June 10, a press conference was organised on the ramp at the JFK facility. Photos Cyril Morris

USA for Africa: making it work. The airline carried out a seamless relief operation with key contributors, including Roger Peake overseeing planning from Los Angeles to Addis Ababa. Charter Operations Supervisors Vince Buscarino managed operations at New York JFK, while Jochem Derschow and Yves Devillars joined the flight from Brussels to Addis Ababa. Flight attendants Jocelyn Dyels and Nancy Gilbert covered LAX-BRU; Lisa Martin and Kristi Peake managed BRU-ADD. The flight crews included Captain Merle Kleen, First Officer James Wilson and Second Officer James Straw for LAX-JFK, Captain Nick Bouja, First Officer Ralph Jarvis and Second Officer Stephen Freeman for JFK-BRU, and Captain Bob Poindexter, First Officer Mick O'Connor and Second Officer John Brown for Brussels-Khartoum and Addis Ababa. Flight attendants Kristi Peake at left and Lisa Martin are seen with security officers at Khartoum Airport.

Second pax 747. A second 747 passenger aircraft was introduced to Flying Tigers' fleet in conjunction with the airline's Military Airlift Command business. The former Air Canada 747-133, leased from GPA Leasing, was delivered in September 1985 and began operations in October after being reconfigured to MAC specifications by maintenance personnel at Tigers' HQ. The fuselage and tail were adorned with Flying Tigers markings, although the fuselage initially retained the Global International Airways red cheatline. The aircraft served both transpacific and transatlantic flights, primarily on U.S./Korea and U.S./Germany routes, accommodating up to 491 passengers, including 30 in the upper deck. The addition to the MAC mission resulted in the recall of 56 furloughed flight attendants. With the inclusion of EI-BPH, Flying Tigers operated two 747s in passenger service from September 1985 to August 1989: LV-MLO, which was in good internal condition, and EI-BPH, which was in disarray internally, with substandard galleys and mismatched passenger seats. Every Tiger flight attendant hoped their assignment would be on MLO rather than the dreaded BPH. Above, EI-BPH is photographed in San Francisco.
Jacques Guillem Collection

Columbus Hub Operation. Boeing 727s and 747s freighters lined up at Flying Tigers' new Columbus, Ohio hub at Rickenbacker Air National Guard Base (LCK). Operations commenced at LCK on March 3, 1986. The new facility was able to accommodate the simultaneous loading and unloading of four 747 and sixteen 727 freighters, plus twenty-six trucks, with remote parking for an additional eleven 747 and 727 aircraft. The hub's 196,000 square-foot cargo sort facility was handling up to seven million pounds of cargo per day and employed 350 people.

Icy in Anchorage. Operations at Flying Tigers' Anchorage terminal, transited by all the airline's scheduled transpacific flights, were particularly challenging during the winter months. Above, 747-245F **N813FT** is being de-iced before departure in March 1986 after a storm left two feet of snow at Anchorage. Gordon Bergman, Anchorage maintenance

Flying Tigers and Benetton team up. For the 1986 Formula One world championship, Flying Tigers partnered with Benetton, sponsoring cars driven by Teo Fabi and Gerhard Berger throughout the season. Flying Tigers served as Benetton's primary transporter for clothing distribution to the US and other major markets, extending their role to the global transportation of racing cars. The Benetton-produced B186 cars, powered by BMW engines, delivered impressive performances on international circuits. With drivers Gerhard Berger and Teo Fabi at the helm, the B186 secured two pole positions, achieved three fastest laps, and claimed victory at the 1986 Mexican Grand Prix.

Liftoff. Flying Tigers 747-245F N813FT, an original Seaboard World aircraft, makes spectacular takeoff from Zurich Airport. As it gets airborne, the main landing gears are already fully tilted, while the (aft) body landing gears are slightly tilted. Both sets are leaving the runway almost simultaneously.
CL44.com Archives

Flying Ferraris. Three valuable Ferrari sports cars were transported from the U.K. to new owners in the U.S. via Flying Tigers' scheduled 747 service from London Heathrow Airport in August 1986. They comprised a prototype Ferrari Testa Rossa racing car, one of only two manufactured by the company in 1961; a 1986 version of the Testa Rossa, seen above, particularly noteworthy because it was painted black instead of the typical Testa Rossa ("redhead") red; and one of the original Ferrari GTO sports cars, constructed in 1963 but left forgotten in a barn for 16 years before being rediscovered and refurbished. Brenard Press Ltd.

Circle T is back. An old favourite returned on January 1, 1987 when Flying Tigers' reintroduced the distinctive Circle T logo that had adorned its aircraft tails for fifteen years from 1961 to 1976. Boeing 747-245F N814FT debuted the new Circle T on its vertical stabilizer as it came out of repainting and routine maintenance at the Los Angeles maintenance facility. In addition, the Flying Tigers lettering had been enlarged on the fuselage for greater visibility and the American flag moved to the rear of the fuselage. That year, the pilots' in-house journal had published an open letter to Stephen M. Wolf, Flying Tigers chairman, president and CEO, suggesting the "much favoured" Circle T should be returned, reasoning that the change would mark the end of five tough years in which the airline's losses averaged $74,600 a day. The letter posed the question, "What better way to declare the era… over?"

Flying barn's close shave. At approximately 7 a.m. local time on January 26, 1987, N820FT, a 747-123F slid off an icy taxiway near the departure end of runway 6R at Anchorage while attempting to turn from taxiway Kilo to taxiway Juliet. The number two engine, a JT9D-7A, sustained significant damage during the low-speed slide over the embankment but fortunately, there were no injuries to the crew, deadheading personnel, or the 120 cows on board. Airbags were used to lift the aircraft's nose so the livestock could be offloaded. The plane was then towed back to the ramp for repairs but no further serious damage was found. The NTSB classified the event as an "incident". Flying Tigers 5001, on a cattle charter from San Francisco to Nagoya, Japan, was in its second leg with a planned takeoff weight just below the Maximum Structural Takeoff Weight. Captain R. Patterson, First Officer A. Kressel and Second Officer Tim Seitz were not held responsible, and the captain attributed the taxiway excursion to patches of ice in the aircraft logbook. Doug Shaw

DC-8-73s join fleet. While none of the airline's DC-8-60s had been redelivered as Super Seventies by the end of 1986, a lease agreement with Guinness Peat Aviation for six DC-8-73CF freighters was announced in January 1987 Stephen M. Wolf, Flying Tigers' chairman, president, and chief executive officer. At the same time, 85 furloughed pilots were recalled, and a recruitment drive added approximately 150 pilots to the books. Over the course of nearly eleven months 550 pilots received DC-8-70 training or were upgraded to positions on the company's 747 and 727. The six DC-8-73CFs, formerly operated by Transamerica Airlines, were delivered between January and March 1987. Above, the first example delivered to Flying Tigers, N4869T, is seen freshly painted with the reintroduced Circle T logo on the tail and ready for delivery at Pinal Air Park, Arizona. It operated its inaugural flight on a Houston-Dallas/Fort Worth-Columbus routing on Friday January 23, 1987. The aircraft then entered transatlantic service over the weekend, transporting cargo to Europe and returning on January 26. The aircraft was re-registered as N701FT in April 1988.

Marine animal charter. More marine animals, including a killer whale, were loaded aboard a Flying Tigers 747 in 1987 destined for SeaWorld amusement parks in Aurora, Ohio and Orlando, Florida. On March 9, 747-249F N807FT "Thomas Haywood" was initially ferried as flight 9116 from Los Angeles to San Diego, under the command of Captain Charles "Chuck" Culver, First Officer James E. Handsaker and Second Officer Robert X. Lane. Two hours and forty minutes later, after completing the loading process, the aircraft left for Cleveland as flight 5116, with a sector duration of four hours and thirty minutes. The animals were on their way from their winter residence in San Diego to SeaWorld's park in Aurora for the summer. The following day, the crew ferried the aircraft as flight 9118 to Orlando for another marine animal transport. It subsequently returned to Cleveland as flight 5119. The photo above captures preparations for loading the large container in Orlando, with the flight crew observing the delicate operation.

Around-the-World. On April 10, 1987, Flying Tigers and Canadian Airlines (formerly CP Air) jointly inaugurated a scheduled round-the-world 747 freighter service. This collaboration granted Flying Tigers access to Canada's scheduled service market and marked the first time two major air carriers from different countries shared resources to offer a global air cargo service. The weekly flight routed Hong Kong, Seoul, Anchorage, Montreal, New York, London, Brussels, Dubai, Bangkok, and back to Hong Kong. Both companies shared aircraft capacity equally while independently competing for payloads along the route. A picture taken in Hong Kong depicts a 747-100F aircraft.

First DC-8-73CF with Tiger crew. Cockpit crews began operating the company's fleet of DC-8-73CFs on August 17, 1987. The inaugural flight marked the completion of an intensive programme at the Samuel B. Mosher Training Centre. Approximately 600 upgraded, recalled and newly hired pilots underwent training for all three types of the airline's aircraft, responding to the addition of six stretched DC-8s and increased 747 and 727 flying. The first DC-8-73CF flight #274 followed a scheduled route from Los Angeles to San Francisco, Columbus, Chicago and Minneapolis. Flying Tigers' officials were at the Los Angeles HQ to meet with the crew members. From left to right: Ron Marasco (Senior Vice President-Operations), Captain Bob Taylor, Chairman Stephen Wolf, Check Captain Art Vance, Check Second Officer Alvin Hader and Captain Donald Pritchett (Vice President Flight Operations), standing in front of N701FT just prior to departure.

Turbulent tales. Flying Tigers 747-249F N807FT "Thomas Haywood" sustained substantial damage when it skidded off a rain-soaked runway at Chicago's O'Hare airport at about 10 a.m. on August 22, 1987. The jet aborted takeoff and skidded off the runway into a muddy field but there were no injuries. Airport ground crew and Chicago fire fighters retrieved the stricken aircraft the following day by creating a wooden road out of planks to get it as far as the runway. A motorised vehicle called a "donkey" then hoisted the jet back onto the runway. On February 19, 1989 N807FT tragically crashed into a hillside on approach to Kuala Lumpur.

International Hub Operations. Boeing 727s and 747s freighters lined up at Flying Tigers' hub in Columbus, Ohio, located at the Rickenbacker Air National Guard Base (LCK). It was officially designated as a Foreign Trade Zone (FTZ) on March 20, 1987. A FTZ is a secured area within the United States that is considered legally outside U.S. Customs territory. The main benefit of operating within an FTZ is the deferment of duty payments for goods imported into the U.S. for assembly or processing. It also provided U.S. Customs inspectors exclusively assigned to oversee Flying Tigers' international hub operations.

First female captain. Sandy Szigeti created history on October 5, 1987 when she became Flying Tigers' first (and only) female captain. Having developed a love of flying at the age of 13, her diverse career spanned skydiving, nursing and almost a decade with the airline. Though a wife and mother, Szigeti pursued her dream of flying, first becoming an air ambulance pilot. After joining Flying Tigers, she rose from first-year pay to 727 captain in just 9 1/2 years. Building on a family tradition, husband Captain Oscar Szigeti and brothers-in-law Jon and David Szigeti are all Tiger pilots. Her achievement inspired other women hopeful of pursuing this great career.

EI-BPH transformation. Following feedback from Flying Tigers' flight attendants, a programme was initiated to significantly improve the passenger cabin of aircraft #890 (EI-BPH), one of the two 747s leased to Flying Tigers for its military contract flights. Between July and November 1987 the airline, together with lessor Guinness Peat Aviation, carried out extensive modifications to the jet. Passenger seats were refurbished and reupholstered, fresh carpeting was fitted and a new movie system was installed. Further enhancements were implemented in the galleys, with ovens, coffeemakers, carts, storage compartment equipment and lavatory areas all upgraded during scheduled checks at Oakland, Los Angeles and Hong Kong. By the end of November 1987, EI-BPH was adorned in Flying Tigers' distinctive colours – its transformation is evident in the above pictures taken in Hong Kong.

Renovated aircraft #890. With aircraft #890 (EI-BPH) comprehensively refurbished inside and out several Tigresses took the opportunity to inspect the improvements first hand. From left to right: flight attendants Jone Amaral, Kristi Peake, Carolyn Inglis, Mary Schulte, Carol Everhart, Betty Carver, Debbie Butcher, Director of Inflight Services Marge Hough, flight attendants Molly Monahan, Geri Lange, Patti Keown, Erlina Baliukas and Andarin Arvola. Gary Watson

20th 747 freighter. Prompted by expected robust demand for global long-range widebody airfreight in the fourth quarter of 1988, and planned expansion of its Asia-to-Europe business in 1989, Flying Tigers acquired its 20th 747 freighter. The aircraft was purchased from Avianca, the Colombian national flag carrier, in August 1988. Boeing 747-124SF N822FT had actually been leased to Flying Tigers (as N809FT) from July 1978 and returned to World Airways two years later. Purchased outright, the 18-year-old jet joined Flying Tigers' global service on September 1, 1988. It is seen in Hong Kong with its new registration N822FT. Below, following conversion and with a light grey colour scheme replacing the classic metallic fuselage, the aircraft showcases its new look.

Fred Reeves Archives

Tiger tails. Three Boeing 747s, including 747-245F N813FT, 747-249F N807FT, and 747-287B LV-MLO, observed at Flying Tigers' headquarters in Los Angeles on September 10, 1988.
George W. Hamlin

Boeing 747-132F N803FT, 747-245F N815FT, and 747-124F N822FT, were sighted at the cargo terminal of Flying Tigers in Anchorage in 1988. Jacques Guillem Collection

Kuala Lumpur tragedy: safety impact. On February 19, 1989, Flying Tigers flight 66 was en route from Singapore to Hong Kong with a planned stop in Kuala Lumpur. Boeing 747-249F, N807FT "Thomas Haywood", under the command of Captain Frank W. Halpin, with First Officer John "Jack" Robinson, Second Officer Ron Penton and mechanic Leonard Walter Sulewski, crashed about 9.8 nautical miles short of the runway at Kuala Lumpur International, killing all four on board. Accident investigators cited the probable cause was the non-standard phraseology used by Kuala Lumpur ATC "causing the crew to misinterpret instructions". Critical alerts from the Ground Proximity Warning System were ignored by crew, and the first officer complained he did not have access to approach charts – his concerns about the chosen approach were also disregarded by the captain. This accident flagged up deficiencies in crew resource management and instrument approach procedures. Subsequently, the GPWS escape manoeuvre was developed, and there was a renewed emphasis on crew training and standard operating procedures. It remains a subject of study for aviation safety, with the original cockpit voice recorder transcript used for training and lessons in improving techniques.

Kuala Lumpur tragedy: commemorating loss. Rare photographs of the crash site, provided by Jack Springer, unveil the solemn scene atop a hill in tranquil Puchong Jaya, Malaysia. Here, the accident investigation committee, comprising members from the Flying Tiger community and the NTSB, gathered for their initial assessment. The modest 481-foot hill, cloaked in dense jungle foliage, presented a daunting obstacle following a gruelling 26-hour journey. Undeterred by the sweltering 100-degree F temperature, they pressed onward. The aircraft's tail bearing the distinctive Circle T logo lay strewn across a jungle path. Among the investigators was Chief Pilot and Director of Flight Operations, Douglas Happ, who confronted the heart-wrenching task of recovering his fallen comrades. In tribute to those lost in the crash, Doug collected up to 43 fan blades, mounting them on a wooden base to create plaques commemorating the tragic event for those involved in the investigation and the four bereaved families.   Jack Springer

Seen at Tokyo Narita in late 1989, N806FT "Robert W. Prescott" stood as the sole Boeing 747 painted in complete Federal Express livery.
Christian Volpati Collection

T-Day. On December 16, 1988, Federal Express announced its intention to acquire Tiger International, Inc. The merger was completed on August 7, 1989, also referred to as T-Day. FedEx added approximately 6,000 employees to its worldwide ranks of 71,500 workers and the deal marked a significant turning point for the company, ushering in a new era of unparalleled global expansion. It secured 11 international route approvals, utilising landing rights obtained through the Flying Tigers' purchase, including destinations in New Zealand, Singapore, Switzerland, Iceland, Ireland, South Korea, the United Kingdom, France, Taiwan, Hong Kong and Malaysia. In Japan, FedEx obtained six 747 parking slots at Tokyo Narita, enabling it to transport freight to Far Eastern destinations that its jets had not previously served. Following a comprehensive reorganisation, Federal Express became the world's largest, full-service, all-cargo airline, boasting a fleet of 108 Boeing 727s, 24 DC-10s, 20 Boeing 747s and 6 Douglas DC-8s. The majority of Flying Tigers' 747s remained in service with FedEx but they were gradually decommissioned up to December 1996. Among them, only N806FT was fully repainted in Federal Express livery following the merger, while retaining its original name, "Robert W. Prescott" in a nod to the Flying Tigers founder. The remaining 747s sported a simplified livery with small decals. For instance, N641FE (formerly N812FT) featured a purple tail with prominent titles, as illustrated in the above image taken at Amsterdam Schiphol in May 1996.
Guy Van Herbruggen Collection

FedEx's passenger services. Following the acquisition of Flying Tigers, Federal Express undertook passenger services, employing nearly 250 flight attendants for three 747 jumbos dedicated to transporting US military personnel and their families to Japan, South Korea, the Philippines and Europe. A new FedEx Air Charter division was created. Unfortunately, these charter operations were gradually phased out as the 747 passenger aircraft were retired from the fleet. The final passenger flight took place on September 30, 1992 with 747-133 N621FE, from Los Angeles to Saint Louis, followed by a repositioning leg back to LAX the next day marking the conclusion of the venture. Guy Van Herbruggen Collection

About the Flying Tiger Line Historical Society

Current FTLHS archives in Los Angeles, California.

In 2023, former Flying Tigers employees joined forces to establish the Flying Tiger Line Historical Society (FTLHS), a registered 501(c)(3) organisation based in California. The FTLHS, as a non-profit entity, is dedicated to preserving the rich history of the Flying Tiger Line and safeguarding its extensive archives, which include documents, photographs, films, and memorabilia.

Originally housed in two back rooms of the former FedEx maintenance hangar building at 7401 World Way West, Los Angeles International Airport, these archives have been preserved by former employees for over 35 years, reflecting their enduring loyalty and passion for their beloved airline.

With the LAX hangar closure in December 2023, the FTLHS has secured a new location near the airport and is actively digitising the archives, creating an accessible online repository for aviation students and enthusiasts, illuminating Flying Tiger's significant role on the global aviation stage. Fundraising is paramount for the FTLHS to build, maintain, and expand the archives, ensuring a lasting legacy.

For further information and to support our mission, please visit www.FTLHS.org or make donations payable to FTLHS and send to P.O. Box 91296, Los Angeles, CA 90009. Contact us via email at contact@FTLHS.org.